# FERMENTED FOODS for everyday eating

T0006853

# FERMENTED FOODS for everyday eating

## DELICIOUSLY EASY RECIPES
## TO BOOST BODY & MIND

RYLAND PETERS & SMALL
LONDON • NEW YORK

**Senior Designer** Toni Kay
**Senior Editor** Abi Waters
**Editorial Director** Julia Charles
**Head of Production** Patricia Harrington
**Creative Director** Leslie Harrington

**Indexer** Hilary Bird

First published in 2024 by
Ryland Peters & Small
20–21 Jockey's Fields
London WC1R 4BW
and
341 E 116th St
New York NY 10029
www.rylandpeters.com

10 9 8 7 6 5 4 3 2 1

Text copyright © Val Aikman-Smith,
Louise Avery, Chloe Coker, Megan
Davies, Amy Ruth Finegold, Tonia
George, Dunja Gulin, Jenny Linford,
Theo A. Michaels, Jane Montgomery,
James Porter, Shelagh Ryan 2024
(see also page 160 for full credits)
Design and photography copyright
© Ryland Peters & Small 2024

ISBN: 978-1-78879-580-7

The authors' moral rights have been
asserted. All rights reserved. No part
of this publication may be reproduced,
stored in a retrieval system, or
transmitted in any form or by any
means, electronic, mechanical,
photocopying, or otherwise, without
the prior permission of the publisher.

A CIP record for this book is available
from the British Library.

US Library of Congress cataloging-in-
publication data has been applied for.

Printed and bound in China

**NOTES**
• Both American (Imperial plus
US cups) and British (Metric)
measurements and ingredients are
included in these recipes for your
convenience; however, it is important
to work with one set of measurements
and not alternate between the two
within a recipe.
• All spoon measurements are level
unless otherwise specified.
• When a recipe calls for the zest of
citrus fruit, buy unwaxed fruit and
wash well before using. If you can
only find treated fruit, scrub
well in warm soapy water
before using.

• Ovens should be preheated
to the specified temperatures.
We recommend using an oven
thermometer.
• Sterilize preserving jars before use.
Wash them in hot, soapy water and
rinse in boiling water. Place in a large
saucepan and then cover with hot
water. With the lid on, bring the water
to the boil and continue boiling for
15 minutes. Turn off the heat, then
leave the jars in the hot water until
just before they are to be filled. Invert
the jars onto clean paper towels to
dry. Sterilize the lids for 5 minutes,
by boiling, or according to the
manufacturer's instructions. Jars
should be filled and sealed while
they are still hot.

# CONTENTS

INTRODUCTION 6

## THE FERMENTED KITCHEN 8

## BREAKFAST & BRUNCH 42

## SOUPS, SALADS & LIGHT LUNCHES 60

## MAIN DISHES 100

## DESSERTS & BAKES 126

## DRINKS 144

INDEX 158

CREDITS 160

# INTRODUCTION

It's thought that gut health can affect lots of different aspects of your health. Your gut is where your body digests food, absorbs energy and nutrients, and gets rid of waste products. It contains trillions of tiny bacteria and other microorganisms, but unlike harmful bacteria that can cause illness, the natural bacteria found in your gut are actually good for you. One of the best things you can do to look after your gut health is to eat a balanced and varied diet which includes plenty of fruit, vegetables and wholegrains. It can also be helpful to introduce the 'live' bacteria found in fermented foods. Fermented foods are highly nutritious and easier to digest than the same foods eaten in their raw or cooked state. They are so nutritious because beneficial microorganisms that

are involved in the fermentation process add live enzymes, B vitamins and protein to the food. Fermentation also increases the bioavailability of minerals present in food, helping the body to assimilate more nutrition. The microorganisms break down complex proteins, carbohydrates and fats into more easily assimilated molecules. Therefore, since healthy gut flora plays a key role in absorption, our body is able to absorb the maximum amount of nutrients, preventing nutrient deficiencies that are so common today.

Fermented foods are highly digestible because good bacteria pre-digest the food, and also because beneficial cultures supply additional enzymes to assist with the digestive process so that our digestive system doesn't have as much work to do. So, we could say that helping digestion, absorption and adding nutrition are the most well-known health promoting properties of fermented foods. Apart from aiding digestion, the lactic-acid bacteria present in fermented foods also alter the pH in the intestines, and a balanced pH in the intestines has been associated with long life and good health. Also, the same lactic-acid bacteria create omega-3 fatty acids, essential for immune system function, which brings us to another very important health benefit of fermented foods – they strengthen our immune system! So, while enjoying a home-made kombucha or home-fermented kefir cream cheese spread over a slice of sourdough bread, you are actually building a resistant immune system that will help you fight disease. In the era when antibiotics are so frequently prescribed and gut flora is so frequently damaged, fermented foods replenish the microflora of the gut.

Improved digestion brings many other benefits, such as digestive comfort, regular bowel movement, better sleep, healthy and radiant skin, increased energy levels, loss of excess weight, possible decrease of sugar cravings, normalization of blood pressure levels, acid reflux and heartburn control, decrease of inflammation in the bloodstream, and candida-overgrowth control, among other things. While all this might sound amazing and the answer to many of our health problems, remember that we are all different, and while a glass of kefir a day might help in controlling the acid reflux for one person, it might not be so effective for someone else. That is why it is important to include different types of fermented foods and drinks into our diets and see which of them agree with us and which do not.

Recent research suggests there is also a link between your gut and your brain. This is sometimes known as the mind-gut connection, the brain-gut connection, or the gut-brain axis. Some digestive conditions, such as IBS, are now thought to be linked with both anxiety and depression and studies suggest that changing your gut bacteria could influence your mood.

The aim of this book is to help you understand and appreciate the benefits of consuming fermented foods and to demonstrate how easy it is to introduce more of them into your daily diet to enjoy better gut health. You can do this by either making simple fermented foods at home and/or buying them ready-made and using them in delicious recipes. If you want to make your own fermented dairy products, the recipes on pages 12–23 will show you how, with foolproof techniques on a range of buttermilk to a feta-style cheese. A sourdough starter and loaf recipe has been included, or simply get into the habit of buying good-quality sourdough bread on a weekly basis. Fermented probiotic drinks such as kefir and

kombucha are available to buy these days but can be expensive so if you do develop a liking for them, learning how to make your own can be a great idea (see pages 26–29). Fermented vegetables have become popular, most notably the Korean pickle kimchi (see pages 30–41) for an achievable kimchi recipe, as well as other simple and versatile pickles to make. Japanese miso is produced by the fermentation of soybeans/soya beans and takes months or even years to mature, and the lengthy aging acts as an external digestive system, making it much easier for us to digest. It is not practical to make it at home but introducing it to simple recipes and dressings is a great way to enjoy the benefits it has to offer (see page 40–41).

Use the information and recipes in this book to embark on your own gut health journey today, at your own pace, and the benefits of improved physical and mental well-being will follow.

# THE FERMENTED KITCHEN

# BUTTERMILK

This useful dairy ingredient, with its delicately thick texture and faint sour tang, can be made very simply at home by triggering a 'ripening' process in milk, which causes the milk to thicken and take on a subtle sharpness. All that's needed in order to start this process is either lemon juice or white wine vinegar. Please note that in the US, buttermilk is only so-called if a culture has been added to it; otherwise, it is known as 'sour milk'.

**500 ml/2 cups whole/full-fat milk, at room temperature**
**2 tablespoons white wine vinegar or freshly squeezed lemon juice**
*sterilized glass jar*
*muslin/cheesecloth*
*30-cm/12-in. length of string/twine*

MAKES 500 ML/2 CUPS

Place the room-temperature milk in a large mixing bowl. Add the vinegar or lemon juice and mix them well.

Set the mixture aside for 15 minutes, during which time the milk will thicken slightly and take on a faintly sour tang.

Store the buttermilk in a sterilized jar covered with muslin/cheesecloth tied up with string, in the refrigerator. It will keep for up to 1 week.

# SOUR CREAM

A versatile dairy ingredient, sour or soured cream is very simple indeed to make at home. Do take note, however, that several hours are required for the process of 'souring' to take place. Fortunately, however, the cream can simply be set aside during this time. Single/light cream rather than rich double/heavy cream is the starting point, giving sour cream its characteristic texture. Cultured buttermilk is added and mixed in, triggering a slow process whereby the single/light cream thickens and takes on the subtle sourness that the name 'sour' cream implies.

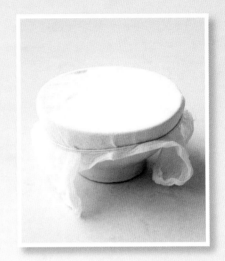

**300 ml/1¼ cups single/light cream**
**3 tablespoons cultured buttermilk**
*muslin/cheesecloth*
*30-cm/12-in. length of string/twine*

MAKES ABOUT 350 ML/1½ CUPS

In a large bowl, mix together the single/light cream and buttermilk.

Cover the bowl with muslin/cheesecloth tied with string and set aside at room temperature for 7–10 hours until thickened. Chill until required.

# CRÈME FRAÎCHE

With its subtle sour tang, crème fraîche is a sophisticated
ingredient, used to add richness to dishes such as savoury
flans, braised dishes and sauces. Despite its luxurious
reputation, crème fraîche is very simple indeed to make
at home – all it needs is time! The starting point for crème
fraîche is smooth textured, butterfat-rich double/heavy
cream. Then, cultured buttermilk is added, which triggers
the process by which the cream thickens and takes on
a slight sharpness.

**300 ml/1½ cups
double/heavy cream**
**3 tablespoons cultured
buttermilk**

MAKES ABOUT
350 ML/1½ CUPS

In a mixing bowl, mix
together the double/heavy
cream and buttermilk.

Cover and set aside at room
temperature for 7–10 hours until
the mixture has thickened. Chill
until required.

# YOGURT

This recipe uses cow's milk, but you can use other milks such goat's milk or sheep's milk. In order to trigger the fermentation process, 'live' yogurt needs to be added, which will be labelled as such on the pot. The yogurt should be incubated in a warm place, such as an insulated cooler box, in which you can place sealed jars of boiled water in order to raise the temperature.

**800 ml/3¾ cups whole/full-fat milk of your choice**
**3 tablespoons 'live' yogurt**
*kitchen thermometer*
*large sterilized jar or a couple of small sterilized jars*

MAKES ABOUT
600 ML/2½ CUPS

Place the milk in a heavy-based saucepan. Heat the milk gently until it reaches 85°C (185°F), checking the temperature with the thermometer. Remove from the heat and allow it to cool for 10–15 minutes until the temperature lowers to 43°C (110°F). Now mix the 'live' yogurt into the warm milk.

Carefully pour the mixture into the sterilized jar or jars. Cover and set aside to incubate in a warm place for 7–8 hours until set to your taste.

The yogurt will keep in a refrigerator for up to 1 week.

# LABNEH

Labneh is a Middle Eastern dairy creation. Sometimes called 'yogurt cheese' it is made very simply by straining yogurt through muslin/cheesecloth overnight. The result is a smooth-textured 'cheese' with a fresh, slightly tangy flavour. Using sheep's or goat's milk yogurt produces labneh that is bright white in colour, with a more pronounced sour tang than labneh made using cow's milk yogurt.

**500 g/2 cups Greek yogurt**
**¼ teaspoon salt (optional)**
*muslin/cheesecloth*
*30-cm/12-in. length of string/twine*
*long wooden spoon*

MAKES ABOUT 350 G/1½ CUPS

Line a large bowl with a square of clean muslin/cheesecloth.

Mix the yogurt and salt (if using) together well. Place the yogurt in the centre of the muslin/cheesecloth square. Wrap the muslin/cheesecloth up around the yogurt and tie it firmly with a long piece of string/twine.

Suspend the muslin/cheesecloth parcel over a deep, large mixing bowl by tying it with the string to a wooden spoon laid across the top of the bowl.

Leave in the fridge for 24 hours. Then, unwrap and use as required.

# RICOTTA

Ricotta is a soft cheese from Italy, used in both savoury and sweet dishes, from pastas to Sicilian cannoli. Traditionally, it was made using the left-over whey from cheese-making, hence its name which means 'cooked again'. In the absence of whey, ricotta can be made very easily using whole/full-fat milk.

**2.8 litres/3 quarts whole/full-fat milk (cow's)**
**3 tablespoons white wine vinegar**
**½ teaspoon salt**
*kitchen thermometer*
*colander*
*wet muslin/cheesecloth*

MAKES APPROX
450–500 G/1¾–2 CUPS

Place the milk in a large, heavy-based saucepan. Heat it slowly and steadily over a medium heat until it reaches 82°C (180°F) on your thermometer.

Remove the milk from the heat and stir in the vinegar and salt at once, mixing thoroughly.

The milk should begin to curdle. Cover and set it aside for 3 hours. Be sure not to move the pan during this time so that the curds will form.

Place a large colander in the sink and line it with a double layer of wet muslin/cheesecloth. Pour the curds into the colander and leave to drain in the sink for 2 hours, so that the excess moisture runs off.

Transfer the ricotta cheese into a bowl and use as required.

# CREAM CHEESE

This recipe involves enriching whole milk both with cream, which gives the cheese a gentle richness of flavour and texture, and 'live' yogurt. It is then heated and later curdled by adding rennet, before being set into curds, cut and drained. This transformation of simple ingredients into a soft cheese is enormously satisfying to make. The freshly made cream cheese will keep in the refrigerator for up to 2 weeks.

**600 ml/2½ cups whole/ full-fat milk**

**400 ml/1⅔ cups double/ heavy cream**

**100 ml/scant ½ cup 'live' yogurt**

**5 drops of cheese-making rennet, dissolved in a little previously boiled and cooled water**

**salt**

*kitchen thermometer*
*shallow, slotted spoon*
*muslin/cheesecloth*
*colander*
*30-cm/12-in. length of string/twine*

MAKES 200–300 G/ 1–1⅓ CUPS, DEPENDING ON DRAINING TIME

Mix together the milk, cream and yogurt in a large, heavy-based saucepan. Gently heat the mixture to 100°F (38°C), checking it with a thermometer. Then, remove from the heat and stir in the rennet mixture and the salt. Stir for 2–3 minutes during which time the milk will begin to curdle. Cover the saucepan with a lid and set aside for 1 hour until the curd has set.

Using a shallow, slotted spoon, cut through the mixture right down to the bottom of the pan. Make this first 'cut' in the centre of the pan, then perform the same movement at roughly 2.5 cm/1 in. intervals to the left and right of the centre until you

reach both edges of the pan. This will allow the curds to separate from the whey. Using the same spoon, carefully remove the curds from the pan, draining off the whey as you do so.

Place the curds in a muslin-/ cheesecloth-lined colander standing on a deep plate. Gather the muslin/ cheesecloth together and squeeze the curds to drain off excess whey. Tie the muslin/cheesecloth with string/twine and suspend the parcel over the colander by attaching string to a long wooden spoon placed across the colander's rim. Leave for at least 8 hours to drain. Remove the cheese from the muslin/cheesecloth, add a little salt and mix in well.

# COTTAGE CHEESE

Cottage cheese retains some moisture after it's been made, which accounts for its characteristic texture. When making it at home, you can experiment by using milks with different fat contents which will alter its flavour and richness.

Gently heat the milk in a large, heavy-based saucepan to 35°C (95°F), using the kitchen thermometer to check the temperature.

Mix the rennet into the cooled water and add it to the warm milk, stirring in thoroughly to disperse it well. Add in the buttermilk and stir in.

Cover with a lid and leave to stand for 1 hour at room temperature so that the mixture coagulates, forming a soft curd.

Using a large knife, cut the curd in the pan into roughly 2.5 cm/1 in. chunks.

Gently heat the curds to 43°C (110°F) and keep them at this temperature, stirring often, for 10 minutes.

Ladle the curds into a muslin-/cheesecloth-lined colander in the sink, and allow them to drain for 3–5 minutes.

Rinse the curds well under cold water, then fold up the muslin/cheesecloth around the curds and twist it to release excess water.

Transfer the curds into a shallow bowl and season with salt to taste, mixing in thoroughly. Cover and chill until required.

**2 litres/2 quarts semi-skimmed/ low-fat milk**
**5 drops liquid cheese-making rennet**
**2 tablespoons previously boiled water, cooled**
**2 tablespoons cultured buttermilk**
**salt, to taste**

*kitchen thermometer*
*large knife*
*ladle*
*muslin/cheesecloth*
*colander*

MAKES ABOUT
350 G/1½ CUPS

# MASCARPONE

This soft, rich cheese is made from two types of cream. Although making mascarpone isn't complex it does require draining time, so factor this in when you're thinking of making and using it.

**450 ml/2 cups single/
light cream
150 ml/²/₃ cup double/
heavy cream
2 drops liquid
cheesemaking rennet
1 tablespoon previously
boiled water, cooled**

*kitchen thermometer
muslin/cheesecloth
colander*

MAKES ABOUT
320 G/1⅓ CUPS

Place both the single/light and double/heavy creamsin heavy-based saucepan.

Heat the mixture gently, stirring now and then, until it reaches 82°C (180°F) on the thermometer.

In a bowl, mix together the rennet and water. Add this diluted rennet to the hot cream and stir for 10 minutes, maintaining the temperature at 82°C (180°F).

Pour the hot cream mixture into a muslin/ cheesecloth-lined colander in the sink, cover, and leave there to drain and cool for 1 hour.

Now place the colander with the cream mixture over a bowl or in a deep dish and set aside in the fridge for 6–7 hours or overnight.

Transfer the soft, thick, smooth-textured cheese in the colander into a dish, cover and chill until required.

# FETA-STYLE CHEESE

Making your own Greek feta-style cheese at home requires time not only for the cheese to be formed, but also for it to acquire its characteristic salty flavour. The recipe opposite uses cow's milk, which gives a mild flavour. For tangier results, use goat's milk or sheep's milk.

Gently heat the milk in a large, heavy-based saucepan to 31°C (88°F). Add the buttermilk and stir it in thoroughly. Cover and set aside for 1 hour.

Mix the rennet with the cooled water, then add this to the milk mixture, stirring in well to disperse thoroughly. Cover and set aside in a warm place for 1 hour, which will allow the milk to turn into curd.

Using a large knife, cut the fragile curd in the saucepan into approximately 2.5 cm/1 in. cubes. Cover the pan and leave for 30 minutes in a warm place.

Using a slotted spoon, carefully transfer the soft curds to a muslin-/cheesecloth-lined colander in the sink. Wrap the muslin/cheesecloth up around the curd, forming a parcel. Now tie the parcel using string to a long wooden spoon laid across the top of a large,

deep pot or bowl. Place the pot or bowl in the refrigerator to drain for 5 hours.

Unwrap the curd and cut into three even slices. Place the slices in a plastic container, sprinkle the curd generously with salt flakes, put the lid on the container and set aside at room temperature for 24 hours. During this time the salt will dissolve into a solution. Turn the slices over once during this period to ensure even salting.

Remove the cheese slices from the salt solution and rinse under cold water to wash off excess salt. Your feta-style cheese is ready for eating. You can slice or cube it or add flavour by putting it in a sterilized glass jar and then covering in olive oil.

**2 litres/2 quarts whole/full-fat milk**
**2 tablespoons cultured buttermilk**
**10 drops of liquid cheesemaking**
    **rennet**
**2 tablespoons previously boiled**
    **water, cooled**
**6 tablespoons sea salt flakes**
**150 ml/²/₃ cup olive oil (optional)**
*kitchen thermometer*
*large knife*
*slotted spoon*
*muslin/cheesecloth*
*colander*
*30-cm/12-in. length of string*
*plastic container*
*sterilized glass jar (optional)*

MAKES ABOUT 300 G/3⅓ CUPS,
DEPENDING ON DRAINING TIME

# WATER KEFIR

Water kefir grains feed on sugary water or juice and produce a fizzy liquid rich in probiotics. These small translucent granules consist of lactic-acid bacteria and some yeasts, and are actually distinctly different from milk kefir grains (see page 24), even though they share the same name. Like any symbiotic community of bacteria and yeast, water kefir granules need regular feeding in order to survive. Use raw cane sugar, rice syrup, maple syrup or honey diluted in water to feed them, but they will also thrive on agave syrup or any other carbohydrate sweetener, or on any sweet liquid (like fruit juice, coconut water, nut milks, etc.). Granulated white sugar can also be used, but you'll need to add a pinch of unrefined sea salt to help the water kefir ferment effectively. If you or your family members are big soft drink/soda fans, and want to avoid unhealthy commercially made drinks, you can make your own fermented probiotic soft drinks with the help of the water kefir grains. Depending on the sweetener and fruit used, you can make many kinds of soft drink/soda, such as the Refreshing Lemon & Mint Soda on page 147) and enjoy the health benefits at the same time!

**4 tablespoons water kefir grains**
**100 g/½ cup raw cane sugar or other sweetener**
**1 litre/4 cups water, preferably non-chlorinated**
*2 x 1.5-litre/quart jars with tightly fitting lids*
*plastic strainer*
*wooden or plastic spoon*

**MAKES 1 LITRE/QUART**

Put the water kefir grains in one of the jars, add the sweetener and water and stir well. Cover it loosely or seal with the jar lid (sealing the jar to get more fizziness). Keep the jar away from direct sunlight and leave to ferment for 48 hours, stirring it on a couple of occasions during that time. Taste the liquid – it should taste slightly sour. If it's still sweet, leave it to ferment for another 12–24 hours (this might be necessary in winter or when your kitchen temperature is lower than 20°C/68°F). Strain the liquid into a clean jar or bottle, and repeat the feeding process.

This fermented drink can be enjoyed immediately or refrigerated. If you are going to put it in the fridge, it's best to consume it within around 1 week.

# MILK KEFIR

Kefir grains are combinations of yeast and bacteria. They are active, alive and unique and cannot be created in the laboratory. Milk kefir grains feed on lactose and therefore need milk sugar to survive. Since they eat lactose, milk kefir is almost lactose-free, rich in beneficial bacteria and much easier to digest than unfermented milk. Whole/full-fat cow's or goat's milk can both be used with great results but as a general rule, the greater the fat content, the creamier the resulting kefir.

**1 tablespoon kefir grains**
**240 ml/1 cup cow's or goat's milk, at room**
   **temperature**
*720-ml/24-fl. oz. glass jar*
*plastic or nylon mesh strainer*
*paper towel or muslin/cheesecloth*
*rubber band*

MAKES 240 G/1 CUP

Put the kefir grains in the jar. Pour over the milk. Cover the jar with a paper towel or clean muslin/cheesecloth and fix it with a rubber band, or if you want the kefir to be fizzy, tighten the lid. Let rest for 18–24 hours, stirring occasionally. The exact time of fermentation depends on the outside temperature and the strength of the grains. If whey separates from the kefir, it has been fermenting for too long, but that's also OK – just shake it. Strain the kefir from the grains using a non-metal strainer and refrigerate. Or, if the kefir grains have formed big clusters, pick them out with wooden chopsticks. Kefir will thicken slightly with cooling. It will keep in the fridge for weeks!

Place the grains in a clean jar, covering them with another 240 ml/1 cup of milk and repeat the process. The grains will grow and multiply, and after a couple of days you will need to increase the amount of milk and eventually give away some of your grains. For example, if you start with 1 teaspoon of grains and 1 cup of milk within a month you may have 1 cup of big kefir lumps and be fermenting about 1.5 litres/6 cups of milk daily! Eventually I had to start giving away some kefir grains, because I didn't want to make more milk kefir than we could use in a day.

Always use clean utensils and jars, do not expose the grains to high heat, feed them regularly and avoid using any metal equipment when handling kefir grains. If you're taking a short holiday/vacation, put the grains in 240 ml/ 1 cup of milk and refrigerate for up to 10 days before the next feeding. Enjoy kefir on its own, as a nourishing and refreshing drink, or use it in raw, cooked and baked recipes as directed.

# REJUVELAC

Apart from being a fermented liquid which helps to start the fermentation process of other foods (e.g. seeds and nuts for making cheese), rejuvelac is also a great energizing drink, so you can make more and enjoy it as an enzyme-rich refreshment when you need a boost.

Put the spelt berries and water in a jar, cover with a paper towel or muslin/cheesecloth, and store in a warm place for 48 hours, or until fizzy and a little sour. In summer, you can just leave it on a work surface, but in winter you'll need to put it close to a radiator or oven. You can let it ferment at room temperature in winter, but it will take at least a week.

Drain, keep the liquid and discard the berries. Try using rye berries, unhulled millet, buckwheat, even brown rice instead of spelt berries.

**30 g/¼ cup sprouted spelt berries (a tiny white tail is enough)**
**480 ml/2 cups water**

MAKES 480 ML/2 CUPS

# BASIC KOMBUCHA

Kombucha is a fermented drink that has recently gained popularity, though its beneficial properties have been enjoyed in Central and Eastern Europe for some time. It is fermented with the help of a symbiotic colony of bacteria and yeast (SCOBY). Kombuchas need both sugar and caffeine to survive and therefore thrive on sweetened tea. To make kombucha tea at home, you can either use a small piece of kombucha mother, or you can make it out of store-bought, live-cultured plain kombucha drinks. Using a kombucha mother often gives faster results than using a drink.

**960 ml/4 cups water**

**2 tablespoons sencha green tea**
   **(or other green/black tea)**

**100 g/¹/₂ cup raw brown sugar**

**small piece of kombucha mother or 480 ml/**
   **2 cups live-cultured plain kombucha drink**

*1.5-litre/quart glass jar*
*muslin/cheesecloth or paper towel*
*rubber band*

MAKES 240 G/1 CUP

Bring the water to a boil, remove from the heat and add the loose tea or tea bags. Steep for around 10 minutes. Strain the tea into a clean jar, add the sugar and whisk until dissolved. Let cool to room temperature. Add the piece of kombucha mother or the kombucha drink, cover with muslin/cheesecloth or a paper towel and fix with a rubber band.

If using the mother, let it sit for about a week, then check the taste. In case it's still too sweet, let it brew for longer. If using kombucha drink, after the first week check every couple of days; a 'baby' kombucha, or skin, should start forming on the surface of the tea. The brewing time depends on the size of the kombucha piece/strength of the store-bought kombucha and temperature (in winter it will ferment much slower unless kept in a warm place).

Ferment until reaching the desired taste – you can enjoy it mildly sweet or wait a while longer for a sour, fizzy kombucha. When you're happy with the taste, transfer most of the liquid into another jar or bottle and drink or refrigerate. Carefully pour the remaining cooled fresh tea over the mother and leftover liquid. If you're going on holiday/vacation, feed the kombucha with freshly made tea and refrigerate immediately. It will need new feeding in about 30 days.

Make sure you use only clean equipment when handling kombucha. In case mould appears on the surface, or you see anything suspicious going on, throw everything away and start over with a new kombucha. Try drinking a small amount of brewed kombucha a couple of days in a row and see how you feel – some people are sensitive to stimulants like caffeine, or even the smallest amount of alcohol (usually, fermented kombucha contains up to 0.5% alcohol), so it's not a drink for everybody. However, most people enjoy drinking it and it's a much healthier alternative to regular coffee and tea!

# SOURDOUGH STARTER

Making your own starter might seem daunting at first, but it really is very simple. Your only job is to replenish the batter with fresh water and flour once a day for about 2 weeks, and the bacteria and yeasts from your environment will do the rest! The right temperature is important to develop a good starter, so make sure you keep it in a warm spot, anywhere from 20–30°C (68–86°F) will do. Starters develop much faster and are stronger if freshly ground flour is used, because fresh flour is full of enzymes and ferments more easily. If you're not using freshly ground flour, buy high-quality organic rye flour.

**1.35 kg/10⅓ cups rye flour**
**1.6 litres/6¾ cups water**
*wide-mouthed 720-ml/24-fl. oz. jar*
*rubber band*
*paper napkin*

**Day 1**  In a clean jar, mix 60 ml/¼ cup water with 50 g/⅓ cup rye flour. Cover and let sit at room temperature for 24 hours.

**Day 2**  Add the same amount of rye and water to the mixture in the jar, stir well, cover and let sit at room temperature for 24 hours.

**Day 3**  Repeat the procedure from day 2.

**Day 4**  There should be some bubbles visible below the surface of rye batter. Leave 1 tablespoon in the jar and discard the rest. Add to the jar 120 ml/½ cup water and 100 g/¾ cup rye flour. Mix well and let sit for 24 hours.

**Day 5**  Again, discard all but 1 tablespoon of the batter and add to the jar 120 ml/½ cup water and 100 g/¾ cup rye flour. Mix well and let sit for another 24 hours.

**Day 6 and 7**  Repeat the same as day 5. The starter should now be bubbly and increase in volume by ⅓ after 24 hours of fermentation.

**Day 8–13**  Repeat the procedure from day 5. By day 13 your starter should double in volume in 24 hours, or earlier. The batter should be full of bubbles and

have a thick layer of froth on top. These are all signs that your starter is ready for use in baking.

**Day 14**  Discard all but 2 tablespoons of your starter, and feed it with 240 ml/1 cup of water and 200 g/1⅔ cups rye flour. It should double in size in 12 hours. Now you will have plenty of starter that can be used immediately for baking and you only need to save 2 tablespoons of it to keep the sourdough going. Don't forget that, because you will need to start all over again if you have no developed starter left in the jar! When you use the starter, save 2 tablespoons of it, replenish it again with 240 ml/1 cup water and 200 g/1⅔ cups rye flour, stir well and leave in a warm place for 12 hours or until bubbly again. If you use the starter every day to bake fresh bread, repeat this procedure every day. If you use the starter once a week refrigerate it after the replenished starter has fermented for 12 hours and take it out a day before you plan baking (within 1 week of placing it in the fridge), and feed it again as done on day 14. Even if you do not plan on using your starter for longer than a week, you have to keep feeding it once a week, as done on day 14, leaving it to ferment for 12 hours or until bubbly and refrigerating it again. This can go on forever!

# SOURDOUGH BREAD

This is the most traditional and natural way to bake bread and, because of the long and natural fermentation process, sourdough bread is much easier to digest than any other type of bread.

**FOR THE 'SPONGE'**
240 g/1 cup water
260 g/1 cup Sourdough Starter
    (see page 28)
260 g/2 cups wheat or spelt flour

**FOR THE BREAD**
½ teaspoon salt
260 g/2 cups flour of your
    choice (rye, barley, wholemeal/
    whole wheat, etc.)
*450-g/1-lb. loaf pan*

MAKES 1 X 450-G/1-LB. LOAF

In a big bowl whisk all the 'sponge' ingredients thoroughly into a thick batter. Cover with a clean, damp tea/dish towel and let sit in the oven with only the light switched on (i.e. without setting a temperature) for 8–12 hours, or until bubbly.

Add the salt to the sponge and stir well. Add the flour and stir vigorously until the dough is thick and you need to stop stirring and start kneading. Knead the bread on a clean work surface, sprinkling more flour as necessary to prevent sticking. The longer you knead, the better: continue for at least 5 minutes to develop elasticity. Oil a clean bowl, place the dough in it and oil it as well. Cover the bowl with a clean, wet tea/dish towel and allow to sit in the oven with only the light switched on again. The dough is ready when it has increased in size by about 50 per cent, which can be between 8–24 hours.

In order to get a nicely shaped loaf, cut a sheet of parchment paper to fit inside the loaf pan without any creases. Flatten the risen dough slightly (sprinkle a little more flour if necessary), shape into a loaf and transfer into the pan. Let rise in the oven for another 2 hours or so.

Preheat the oven to 220°C (425°F) Gas 8. Place the pan in the middle of the preheated oven, lower the heat to 200°C (400°F) Gas 6 and bake for 1 hour. You can take the bread out of the oven, tip it out of the pan and tap the bottom of the loaf – it should sound hollow. If not, return to the pan and into the oven for another 10 minutes.

Remove from the pan, peel off the parchment paper and let cool slightly before cutting. If you want a softer crust, wrap the warm bread in a clean, damp tea/dish towel and let cool.

To store the sourdough bread, wrap it in a clean, dry tea/dish towel and place inside a paper bag. This bread does not spoil or mould easily, so it can be consumed up to 2 weeks after baking. It will harden, but can be sliced and steamed to soften up before serving.

# FERMENTING VEGETABLES

Out of all the fermented foods and beverages you can make at home, fermenting vegetables is the easiest type of fermentation, and a great way to enter the world of home-fermented foods! There are many different methods of fermenting vegetables across the world, but one thing is certain: whichever method you use, fermented vegetables are very nutritious, so eating them regularly will bring you many health benefits. They are also very tasty and a great addition to your everyday meals! The basic principle of most of vegetable fermenting methods is that vegetables are submerged under liquid and the bacteria native to the vegetables start the fermentation process. Lactic-acid bacteria create an acidic environment in which unwanted organisms cannot survive, protecting vegetables from spoilage. No wonder that lactic-acid fermentation has been historically popular as a food-preservation method, as it is an effective method of preserving vegetables for the colder months of the year when fresh vegetables are not always available. Eating fermented foods also protects against vitamin C deficiency and provides other critical nutrients for a well-balanced diet.

### Dry-salting
This refers to adding salt to chopped vegetables, which are then squeezed or pounded until the salt pulls out the water and the vegetables start sweating. The juice that comes out of the vegetables is then used as a brine in which the vegetables are submerged during the fermentation. See Purple Sauerkraut with Dulse & Caraway Seeds (page 38).

### Brining
This is more suitable for large pieces of vegetables or whole vegetables. They are not salted directly but rather submerged in brine and kept submerged, or even under pressure, for a certain period of time. Brines can also be flavoured with different spices so that the vegetables absorb the spices and become aromatic or strong flavoured. Also, yogurt or kefir whey can be used instead of water to help the fermentation process. See Turmeric & Chilli Kimchi (see page 37).

### Fermenting in miso
A Japanese way of pickling (called miso-zuke in Japanese), this is one of many types of Japanese preserved vegetables or tsukemono. Since miso is a paste, sliced or whole vegetables (most usually roots, garlic, onion, etc.) are layered with miso and completely surrounded by the paste, and left to ferment from anything between a couple of days to up to a couple of years! For an alternative way to enjoy miso see the Spicy Leek & Miso Condiment on page 41.

### Fermenting with shoyu
Another tsukemono (see above), and is possibly the easiest and quickest Japanese pickling technique, similar to brining (see opposite). Vegetables are thinly sliced, mixed with shoyu (Japanese natural soy sauce) and put under pressure for a short period of time (up to 2 hours). Vegetables remain crunchy and the taste is light and refreshing.

# PICKLES

This trio of punchy pickles is closer to the Japanese tsukemono (see page 32) than western-style pickles as they are inspired by Hawaiian cuisine. In most cases they are used to enhance or balance flavours or as a palate cleanser. You can enjoy them with sush, in poke-style rice bowls, alongside cheese and meats as part of a sharing board, as a burger relish or even just on top of cheese on sourdough toastfor an instant tangy flavour hit!

# Cucumber Pickles

2 cucumbers
1 tablespoon salt
120 g/4 oz. hijiki or arame seaweed
235 ml/1 cup rice wine vinegar
180 g/scant 1 cup granulated sugar
1 teaspoon black sesame seeds

SERVES 6

Slice the cucumbers on the diagonal and spread out on a ceramic platter. Mix the salt into the cucumber. Let stand for 10 minutes, then rinse and pat dry.

Place the seaweed in a small bowl and hydrate in a little warm water for 10 minutes, then drain and squeeze out the excess water.

Combine the vinegar and sugar in a medium saucepan with 235 ml/ 1 cup water and bring to the boil. Take off the heat and add the cucumber, seaweed and sesame seeds. Place in a sealable container, making sure the liquid is covering the cucumber, cool down, then refrigerate. Let the flavours mellow for a few days before eating. Consume within 1 month.

# Pickled Scotch Bonnets

500 ml/2¼ cups vinegar – can be
    half white wine vinegar and half
    red wine vinegar
2 tablespoons sugar
2 teaspoons salt
1 teaspoon allspice berries
280 g/10 oz. Scotch Bonnets

MAKES ENOUGH TO FILL A
1-LITRE/1-QUART PRESERVING
JAR

Prepare the pickling solution. Place the vinegar, sugar and salt in a medium pan with 120 ml/½ cup water and boil until the sugar has dissolved. Add the allspice berries.

Carefully cut the tops off the Scotch Bonnets to expose the inside of the peppers to the pickling solution. Place the peppers in a second pan with enough water to cover and bring gently to the boil for no more than 1 minute. Strain the peppers and pack into the jar. Pour over the slightly cooled pickling solution, leaving a 1-cm/½-in. gap at the top. Seal. Let rest for a few days before using to allow the flavours to blend. Will keep for many months stored in the refrigerator.

# Pickled Ginger

250 g/9 oz. fresh ginger –
    try using young ginger
1 tablespoon Maldon sea salt
60 g/5 tablespoons sugar
300 ml/1¼ cups rice wine vinegar
3 tablespoons water
2 drops red food colouring (optional)
    (see Tip)

MAKES ENOUGH TO FILL A
500-ML/17-OZ. PRESERVING JAR

Peel the ginger and slice thinly. Pile into a bowl and rub in the salt. Cover and refrigerate for at least 2 hours. Squeeze the ginger to remove the salt and the liquid, then place the ginger in the preserving jar.

Bring the remaining ingredients to a simmer in a small pan. Make sure the sugar is dissolved. Pour into the jar and cool a little before sealing. Leave undisturbed for at least three days before using. This allows the flavours to mellow and the ginger to have less kick.

# TURMERIC & CHILLI KIMCHI

This is just one of many variations of the South Korean phenomenon kimchi. Take a spoonful or two every day with your main meal to improve digestion. It's worth making plenty at once and using it up within 2 months.

1.2 litres/6 cups cold water
60 g/3 tablespoons sea salt
600 g/7 cups green cabbage,
   cut into thick strips
8 carrots (around 520 g/1 lb. 3 oz.
   (total weight), cut into
   bite-sized pieces
20-g/³⁄₄-oz. piece fresh ginger
4 garlic cloves
4 small whole red chillies/chiles
1 teaspoon turmeric powder
¹⁄₂ teaspoon chilli powder
*pickle press (optional)*

MAKES 300–400 G/3–4 CUPS

Make a brine by mixing the water and salt and stir well.

Put the cabbage and carrots into the pickle press (if using) and cover with the brine. To keep it submerged, screw the lid down just a little. Allow to soak for few hours or overnight. If you don't have a pickle press, put the vegetables in a bowl and weigh them down by resting a plate on top of them. Meanwhile, finely chop the ginger and garlic. Drain the soaked vegetables, reserving the brine. Mix them with the spices and add the chillies/chiles.

Put this mixture back into the pickle press or bowl and add enough brine to rise over the vegetables once you press them down. Screw the lid as much as you can, or, if using a plate, put something heavy on top of it. The vegetables must be submerged in the brine the entire time during fermentation. Check every 2 days and remove any foam or mould spots that might appear on the surface of the brine, which is totally normal. Allow to ferment for a minimum of 1 week but the best taste develops after 4 weeks. When the vegetables are done, transfer into jars, cover with the brine and keep in the fridge.

# PURPLE SAUERKRAUT
## with dulse & caraway seeds

We should always have a rainbow of colours on our plates, and this red cabbage fermented into a purple sauerkraut will brighten up any meal! To boost the mineral intake seaweed has been added here, and spices are also a welcome addition; caraway seeds in this sauerkraut make it very aromatic. Try this combination – you won't be disappointed!

**11¹⁄₂ teaspoons caraway seeds**
**10 g/¹⁄₂ oz. dulse seaweed**
**1 medium head red cabbage,**
    **(around 800 g/28 oz. in weight)**
**2¹⁄₂ teaspoons salt**
*pickle press, clean glass jar or crock*

MAKES 200 G/2 CUPS

Use a pestle and mortar to crush the caraway seeds. Cover the dulse with water and let it soak for 10 minutes. Very finely chop or grate the cabbage. Add the salt and squeeze with clean hands – this will help to release the juices. Add the drained and chopped seaweed and crushed caraway seeds.

The cabbage should be dripping wet. To ensure proper fermentation without the presence of oxygen, carefully pack the spiced cabbage with its juice in a pickle press, a big jar or a crock. It should always be submerged in its own brine, so stuff it tightly and screw down the lid of the pickle press as much as you can, or if using a jar or crock, pack tightly, cover with a plate that fits inside and place some kind of weight on top (like a glass bottle filled with water, a marble weight or a stone).

Check after 12 hours and press again; the cabbage will wilt further and more juice will come out. The shortest fermentation time for the process to start is 3 days, but I usually leave it for at least 7 days and ideally for 4 weeks. During the fermentation, it's necessary to check your press, jar or crock every other day and remove any foam and/or mould that might form on the surface of the brine – a common and normal event that will not, in any way, affect the quality of your sauerkraut.

After 4 weeks transfer the sauerkraut to jars, cover in brine and refrigerate. It will stay fresh for at least 1 month and possibly 2–3 months.

# SPICY LEEK & MISO CONDIMENT

This condiment isn't just tasty, it's good for you, too! Leek, onions and garlic are well known for their therapeutic properties, and if you add olive oil, chilli and miso paste, you will get an aromatic blend rich in probiotics that will strengthen your immune system.

**2 medium leeks**
**2 medium onions**
**1 garlic bulb, cloves crushed**
**5 tablespoons olive oil**
**1 small dried chilli/chile, crushed**
**1–2 tablespoons barley or rice miso**

MAKES 200-300 G/2-3 CUPS

Slice the leeks in half lengthwise and wash thoroughly. Peel the onions and garlic and then finely chop all of the vegetables. Heat the oil in a heavy -based saucepan, and add the finely chopped leek and onion and a pinch of salt. Combine well and cover. Simmer over a low heat until the onion becomes translucent, about 20 minutes, stirring occasionally. Add the chilli and sauté for another minute. Meanwhile, dilute the miso in a little hot water in a bowl.

Remove the saucepan from the heat source, add the diluted miso and crushed garlic cloves and mix well. Add a little more hot water to reach the desired consistency. This condiment is quite sharp and salty – a spoonful of it per day is enough. It's a great addition to grain boiled vegetables. It will keep in the fridge for at least 1 week.

# RICH MISO-TOFU DRESSING

This dressing stays fresh in the fridge for days and adds some extra protein from tofu into your salad or snack. Use leftovers as a dip for raw vegetables and crackers, or as a bread spread when you are making sandwiches.

**200 g/1 cup fresh tofu**
**2 teaspoons barley or rice miso**
**4 teaspoons lemon juice**
**2 teaspoons Dijon mustard**
**3 teaspoons dark sesame oil**
**1/2 teaspoon salt**
**2 tablespoons finely chopped onion**
**60 ml/1/4 cup water**

MAKES 320 G/1½ CUPS

Blend all the ingredients well until the mixture reaches a velvety consistency. Serve immediately or let sit in the fridge overnight before using. Add more water if you prefer a less dense dressing.

# BREAKFAST
# & BRUNCH

# FERMENTED MILLET PORRIDGE

Millet is an amazing grass and grain that is highly underestimated nowadays. It is very rich in copper, phosphorus, manganese and magnesium – a veritable mountain of minerals! Serve with sunflower seeds, and a spoonful or two of fermented vegetables or a fermented condiment, and this basic recipe becomes a tasty, satisfying savoury breakfast, packed full of nutrients. Note you'll need to soak the millet for 2–3 days before you can prepare this recipe.

100 g/½ cup millet

480 ml/2 cups water

2 tablespoons yogurt whey (the yellowish liquid that sits on top of your yogurt)

½ umeboshi plum or ⅛ teaspoon salt

2 tablespoons dry-roasted sunflower seeds

1 teaspoon soy sauce

*720-ml/24-fl. oz. glass jar*

*muslin/cheesecloth or paper towel*

SERVES 1-2

Put the millet in a sieve/strainer and wash well under running water. Drain and put in the jar. Pour over the water and add 2 tablespoons of whey. Cover with muslin/cheesecloth or a paper towel and fix with a rubber band. Let soak for 2–3 days at room temperature and stir at least once a day. The whey will speed up the fermentation process but it can also be omitted if desired.

Put the soaked millet, together with the soaking water, in a small saucepan. Bring to the boil over a medium heat. Stir occasionally to prevent burning and boiling over. Add the umeboshi plum or salt and simmer, half-covered, for about 20 minutes. Add more hot water during the cooking, if necessary, to get a creamy porridge/oatmeal.

Wash and drain the sunflower seeds (this will prevent them from burning) and dry-roast in a frying pan/skillet over a medium heat, stirring constantly until the seeds start sizzling, at which point they will release their aroma, become golden brown and puff up. Transfer to a bowl and add the soy sauce. Mix until the hot seeds absorb all the soy sauce and become dry and crunchy. Sprinkle the seeds over the warm porridge/oatmeal and serve with the toppings of your choice.

# BEETROOT LATKES
## with smoked salmon & crème fraîche

Serve this strikingly colourful dish as a satisfying brunch plate. Cool, silky crème fraîche contrasts well with salty smoked salmon and the slightly sweet, earthy-tasting, crisp-textured beet(root) latkes.

150 g/5 oz. raw beet(root)
150 g/5 oz. potatoes, peeled
1/2 red onion, peeled
1 egg, beaten
50 g/1/2 cup medium matzo meal
sunflower oil, for frying
200 g/61/2 oz. smoked salmon
4 dollops of crème fraîche
    (see page 12)
salt and freshly ground
    black pepper, to season
snipped chives, to garnish
*baking sheet lined with
    parchment paper*

SERVES 4

Peel the beet(root) and trim off the trailing root. Hold each beet(root) by the stalk end and grate them coarsely. Grate the potato and the red onion.

In a large bowl, mix together the grated beet(root), potato and onion. Add in the egg, matzo meal, salt and pepper to taste and mix together thoroughly to form a thick, sticky mixture.

Preheat the oven to 140°C fan/160°C/325°F/gas 2.

Pour the oil to a depth of 0.5 cm/1/4 in. into a heavybottomed frying pan/skillet and heat it up thoroughly.

Fry the latkes in batches. Add 4 separate spoonfuls of the mixture, spaced well apart, to the hot oil, pressing each down lightly with the spoon to spread it out. Fry them for 3 minutes, then flip each one over and fry for a further 2 minutes. Carefully remove the fried latkes from the pan and onto the prepared baking sheet before placing them in the oven to keep warm.

Repeat the process four times, making 12 latkes in all.

Serve the beet(root) latkes with smoked salmon and a dollop of crème fraîche topped with chopped chives.

# MAPLE-SESAME BACON & CREAM CHEESE BAGELS

There's no better way to enjoy your homemade cream cheese than on toasted sourdough bagels, topped with deliciously easy maple-sesame bacon.

1 teaspoon sesame seeds
6 rashers/slices smoked
    streaky bacon
2 sourdough bagels
1 tablespoon maple syrup
100 g/½ cup cream cheese
    (see page 16)
salt and freshly ground
    black pepper
vegetable oil, for frying

SERVES 2

Heat a large, non-stick frying pan/skillet over a medium heat and add the sesame seeds. Let them toast for 3–4 minutes until golden, then transfer to a small bowl and wipe out the pan.

Heat a small drizzle of oil in the pan on a medium-high heat and, once hot, add the bacon. Let it fry, turning occasionally until deep golden brown and crispy, approximately 7–10 minutes.

Meanwhile, halve and toast the bagels, then leave in the toaster to keep warm.

When the bacon is ready, remove from the heat and add the maple syrup and toasted sesame seeds to the pan. As the syrup sizzles, turn the bacon over a couple of times to coat.

Spread the cream cheese onto the bagels, sprinkle over a pinch of seasoning, top with the bacon. Serve immediately.

# SPICY KIMCHI HASH BROWNS
## with poached eggs

**10 large Russet potato, washed
and grated, skin on**

**2 garlic cloves, crushed/minced**

**2 cups/160 g Turmeric & Chilli Kimchi
(see page 37) or any store-bought
kimchi of your choice**

**3 tablespoons olive oil,
plus extra to serve**

**4 eggs**

**1 tablespoon vinegar**

**a bunch of Thai basil or regular
basil, torn**

**a small bunch of flat-leaf parsley, torn**

**salt and freshly ground black pepper,
to season**

**hot sauce of your choice, to serve**

SERVES 1

The fermented kimchi here gives the hash browns crunch and spice. Topped with poached eggs and sprinkled with aromatic herbs, Sunday couldn't get off to a better start.

Place the grated potato, garlic, and kimchi in a large bowl and mix together. Season with salt and pepper.

Heat a large cast-iron skillet/frying pan over medium–high heat and add the olive oil. When the oil starts to sizzle, add the potato-kimchi mix and brown for 2 minutes. Reduce the heat and continue to cook, stirring occasionally, for another 6–8 minutes. You want the hash browns to be crispy and browned.

Crack the eggs into separate small bowls. Fill a medium skillet/frying pan three-quarters of the way up with water. Add a tablespoon of vinegar and place over medium heat until bubbles start to form in the bottom. Carefully pour the eggs one at a time into the water, making sure they are spaced apart. Cook for 4 minutes, then remove with a slotted spoon, gently shaking off any excess water. Rest on a large plate.

Divide the hash browns between 4 plates or serving skillets (as shown) and top each with an egg. Sprinkle with torn Thai basil and parsley leaves. Drizzle with a little olive oil and finish with a sprinkle of salt and pepper. Serve with Texan Hot Sauce for a tangy kick.

# EGGY BREAD with capers & petit pois

This is a more grown-up savoury version of the sort of 'eggy' bread you might have enjoyed as a child, with a pleasing saltiness from the capers (one of the earliest vegetable ferments to come from the Mediterreanan). As this can be rustled up from storecupboard and freezer ingredients so makes a good healthy and hot brunch with little planning.

2 eggs
30 ml/2 tablespoons whole/
    full-fat milk
30 g/2 tablespoons unsalted butter
4 slices sourdough bread
20 g/2 tablespoons capers, drained
100 g/³/₄ cup frozen petit pois or
    garden peas
salt and freshly ground
    black pepper, to season

SERVES 2

Preheat the oven to 100°C fan/120°C/250°F/Gas ½. Place an ovenproof plate on the bottom shelf of the oven.

Whisk the eggs and milk in a shallow bowl with a generous pinch of seasoning. Heat half the butter in a non-stick frying pan/skillet over a medium heat.

Add a slice of bread to the egg bowl and slosh it around so it absorbs some of the egg mixture, then flip it over and slosh around once more.

Once the butter has melted and is gently sizzling in the pan, transfer the eggy bread to the pan and fry for about 3 minutes on each side, until both sides are golden brown and crispy-edged. While the first slice is cooking, place a second piece of bread in the egg bowl to soak.

When the first slice of bread is done, transfer it to the warming plate in the oven and cook the next slice in the same way. Repeat the process until all 4 slices have been cooked. Use the remaining butter as needed.

When the pan is empty, pop the capers and peas straight in, with a small splash of water and twist of pepper. Fry for about 3 minutes, until they're tender and starting to catch a little. As they cook, gently mash them in the pan with the back of a fork. Taste to check for seasoning.

Halve the eggy bread, divide between serving plates, then pile the capers and petit pois on top and serve immediately.

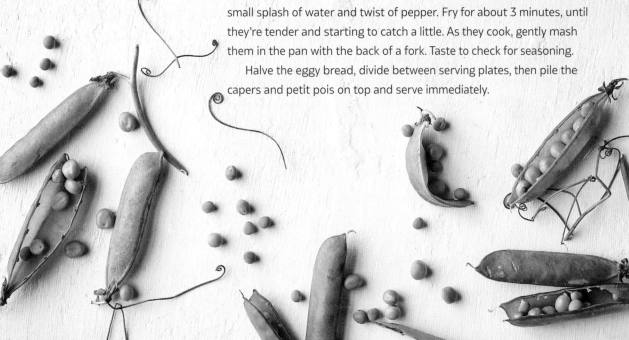

# MISO MUSHROOMS ON TOAST

Miso paste has probiotic properties, so it's great for our immune systems, digestion and gut healthy and it's incredibly moreish too. This makes a deliciously umami breakfast and it's a great way to add a bit of life to any limp mushrooms you may have lurking in your fridge. Do use a good bread for this, something with texture like a spelt or rye sourdough works well.

2 slices sourdough bread
1 lemon
400 g/14 oz. mixed mushrooms,
    sliced
2 large garlic cloves, grated
50 g/1¾ oz. red or white miso paste
30 ml/2 tablespoons water
1 teaspoon sesame oil
10 g/⅓ oz. freshly chopped flat-leaf
    parsley and/or coriander/cilantro
salt and freshly ground
    black pepper, to season
olive oil, for cooking

SERVES 2

Toast the bread (leaving it in the toaster to keep warm) and cut the lemon in half.

Heat a drizzle of oil in a large frying pan/skillet and, once hot, add the mushrooms. Pan-fry for 7–10 minutes, tossing occasionally, until well-browned and tender, but not overcooked.

Next, add the garlic, miso paste, a good squeeze of lemon juice, water and sesame oil and let sizzle, tossing to coat the mushrooms.

Fry for a minute or two, then remove from the heat, add the herbs, and fold through. Taste to check for seasoning, then pile on top of toast and serve. Chop up the leftover lemon and pop a wedge on each plate for squeezing.

# BLACK PEPPER RICOTTA
## & bay-roasted grape sourdough toasts

Compared to most cheeses, ricotta is a healthier choice because it contains less salt and fat. It's light and creamy with a slightly grainy texture and delicate flavour that can be used on its own or in dishes. (See photograph on page 56.)

**5–6 fresh bay leaves**
**300 g/10½ oz. red grapes**
**4 slices sourdough or rye bread**
**250 g/1 cup ricotta (see page 15)**
**½ teaspoon cracked black pepper**
**sea salt flakes**
**olive oil, for drizzling**

SERVES 2-4

Preheat the oven to 210°C fan/230°C/450°F/Gas 8.

Scatter the bay leaves onto a small baking sheet and top with the grapes. Drizzle with some olive oil and a sprinkling of sea salt. Place on the middle shelf of the preheated oven and bake for 15 minutes until the grapes are soft, coloured and the skins are bursting.

Meanwhile, toast the slices of bread, then mix the ricotta with the black pepper and a pinch of salt and pile on top of the toast. Once the grapes are ready, pile on top of the ricotta toast and make sure you pour any pan juices over too.

# BANANA & BLUEBERRY KEFIR MUFFINS

These muffins are not to be missed – very light, juicy and happy to accommodate any fruit you might have that needs using up. Fresh blueberries work particularly well, but raspberries, sour cherries or a mix of any forest fruits can also be used, as can chopped peaches, apricots and plums. The choice of flours is also up to you. This recipe uses some organic coconut flour (not flakes) to lower the gluten amount, but using only unbleached flour with some wholegrain/whole-wheat flour is also an option.

3 tablespoons virgin coconut oil
   or extra virgin olive oil
1 very ripe banana
225 g/³/₄ cup maple syrup
420 ml/1³/₄ cups milk kefir
   (see page 24), at room
   temperature, or store-bought
   kefir, as preferred
¹/₄ teaspoon bourbon vanilla powder
130 g/1 cup unbleached plain/
   all-purpose flour
130 g/1 cup coconut flour
70 g ¹/₂ cup wholegrain/
   whole-wheat flour
¹/₄ teaspoon salt
1 teaspoon baking powder
1 teaspoon bicarbonate of/
   baking soda
150 g/1 cup fresh blueberries
   or other fruit
*12-hole/cup muffin pan*

MAKES 12

Preheat the oven to 160°C fan/180°C/350°F/gas 4.

If necessary, place the jar with coconut oil in a pot of hot water to melt it.

Blend the first four ingredients in an electric blender. This is the wet mixture. Sift all of the remaining ingredients (except for the fruit) into a mixing bowl. This is the dry mixture. Combine the wet and dry ingredients and mix gently with a silicone spatula until just combined. Add 100 g/²/₃ cup of the blueberries and incorporate. Do not overmix.

Oil the muffin moulds or line them with non-stick paper liners. Divide the mixture among the muffin cups. Top each muffin with a couple of the remaining 50 g/¹/₃ cup blueberries. Bake in the preheated oven for about 25 minutes. Allow to cool in the muffin pan for a few minutes, the transfer to a wire rack to cool completely.

These muffins are great for breakfast but also as an afternoon snack with a cup of your favourite tea blend.

# SOUPS, SALADS & LIGHT LUNCHES

# SPINACH YOGURT SOUP
## with caramelized butter

Using your homemade yogurt in this delicately-flavoured soup gives it a subtle tang. For a light meal, serve it with crusty bread.

2 tablespoons olive oil

1 white onion, finely chopped

1 teaspoon ground cumin

$\frac{1}{2}$ teaspoon chilli/hot red pepper flakes

800 ml/3$\frac{1}{4}$ cups chicken or vegetable stock

a small bag of fresh spinach, leaves chopped

175 g/scant 1 cup yogurt (see page 13), or use storebought

1 egg

2 teaspoons plain/allpurpose flour

40 g/3 tablespoons butter

a sprinkling of ground sumac (optional)

salt and freshly ground black pepper, to season

SERVES 4

Heat the olive oil in a large, heavy-based frying pan/skillet. Add the onion and fry gently, stirring often, for 5 minutes, until softened. Sprinkle in the cumin and chilli/hot red pepper flakes and mix together.

Add the stock, season with salt and pepper and bring to the boil, then reduce the heat and simmer gently for 5 minutes.

Meanwhile, caramelize the butter by gently melting it in a small saucepan until a white sediment appears. Continue cooking over a very low heat, stirring now and then, until the white sediment turns brown and the butter has a nutty fragrance.

While the butter is caramelizing, add the spinach to the simmering soup and cook gently for 2–3 minutes.

Meanwhile, whisk together the yogurt, egg and flour until well-mixed. Add the yogurt mixture to the gently simmering soup and continue cooking over a low heat for 3–4 minutes. Stir continuously and make sure that the soup does not come to the boil.

Stir in the caramelized butter, sprinkle with sumac, if desired, and serve at once.

# CHILLED CUCUMBER & MINT SOUP
## with Parmesan crisps

This refreshing chilled soup is perfect for a warm summer's day. If you aren't a fan of chilled soups, give this recipe a try and be converted. It's easy to make in advance and will keep for a day in the fridge, ready to serve. The Parmesan crisps add extra texture but are optional.

6 cucumbers, peeled, cored,
   and chopped into chunks
a small handful of fresh mint,
   roughly chopped
480 ml/2 cups crème fraîche (see
   page 12), or use storebought
freshly grated zest of 1 unwaxed
   lemon and freshly squeezed lemon
   juice, to taste
1¹/₂ garlic cloves, crushed
1 teaspoon sugar
salt and freshly ground black pepper,
   to season

**FOR THE PARMESAN CRISPS
(OPTIONAL)**
50 g/1³/₄ oz. Parmesan cheese,
   finely grated
*baking sheet lined with
   parchment paper*

SERVES 4-6

Preheat the oven to 180°C (350°F) Gas 4.

Put the cucumbers and mint in a food processor and blitz to a purée. Push the purée through a fine mesh sieve/strainer using the back of a ladle — it will look quite watery.

Put half of the pulp left in the sieve/strainer back into the blender along with the watery mixture. Add the crème fraîche/sour cream, lemon zest, garlic, sugar and salt and pepper, then blend until combined. Taste the mixture and season with lemon juice, sugar and salt and pepper. This soup needs to be highly seasoned to bring out the delicate flavours.

To make the crisps, spread thin strips of Parmesan onto the prepared baking sheet. Ensure you leave a good space between each strip as they will spread in the oven.

Bake the crisps in the oven for 7 minutes until the Parmesan melts and colours slightly. Take them out of the oven and gently remove the crisps from the baking sheet using a palette knife. Put the crisps on a rack until cooled and crisp.

Ladle the soup into serving bowls and put an ice cube in each bowl of soup to keep it well chilled. Top with the Parmesan crisps and serve immediately

# CARROT, CORIANDER & CARAWAY SOUP
## with sourdough croutons

Caraway is a delicious and underused spice and it works equally well in both sweet and savoury dishes (see also Purple Sauerkraut on page 38). Here it's paired with the classic combination of carrot and coriander in a warming and comforting soup.

1 white onion, finely chopped

4 garlic cloves, grated

1 tablespoon coriander seeds, crushed

1 tablespoon caraway seeds

650 g/23 oz. carrots, cut into 1-cm/³/₈-inch slices

1.5 litres/6 cups vegetable stock

vegetable oil, for cooking

about 20 g/³/₄ oz. freshly chopped coriander/cilantro, plus extra leaves, to serve

salt and freshly ground black pepper, to season

**FOR THE SOURDOUGH CROUTONS**

2–3 slices sourdough bread

1 tablespoon olive oil

20 g/³/₄ oz. hard cheese (any)

SERVES 4

Preheat the oven to 200°C fan/220°C/425°F/Gas 7.

Heat a generous glug of oil in a large saucepan or casserole/Dutch oven and, once hot, add the onion. Sweat for 5 minutes. Next, add the garlic, coriander seeds and caraway seeds. Fry for 1 minute, until fragrant, then add the carrots. Fry for 5 minutes, stirring often, then add the vegetable stock.

Bring the soup to the boil, then immediately reduce to a simmer. Leave on the hob/stovetop gently bubbling away for 20 minutes.

Meanwhile, tear or cut up the sourdough bread into croutons, place on a baking sheet, drizzle with the olive oil and grate over the cheese. Place on the top shelf of the preheated oven and bake until golden and the cheese has melted, about 10 minutes.

Blitz the soup with a stick blender, taste, season and taste again. Add the fresh coriander/cilantro, then briefly blitz again. Transfer to bowls and top with the croutons, and some extra coriander/cilantro, if you like.

# ASPARAGUS, PEA & LABNEH SALAD

300 g/10 oz. fresh asparagus spears, trimmed

½ tablespoon olive oil

200 g/¾ cup fresh peas or 80 g/ ¾ cup frozen petit pois, thawed

350 g/1½ cups goat's milk or sheep's milk yogurt labneh (see page 14)

25 g/3 tablespoons flaked/slivered almonds

2 teaspoons finely grated lemon zest

fresh flat-leaf parsley, to garnish

salt and freshly ground black pepper, to season

*ridged grill pan*

SERVES 4

The taste of summer on a plate, this simple, vibrant salad can be served as an elegant first course or as an accompaniment to cold meats.

Preheat a ridged stovetop grill pan. Toss the asparagus spears with the olive oil and season with salt and pepper. Dry-fry the asparagus for 2–3 minutes on each side, until lightly charred. Set aside and allow to cool.

Add the almonds to the ridged stovetop grill pan and dry-fry until they're golden brown. Set aside and allow to cool.

Blanch the peas in boiling water for 2 minutes. Then drain, refresh in cold water to stop the cooking process and drain again.

Assemble the salad, by placing the fried asparagus and blanched peas in a serving dish. Top with spoonfuls of labneh, then sprinkle over the toasted almonds and lemon zest. Garnish with flat-leaf parsley leaves and serve at once.

# BROAD BEAN, FETA & DILL SALAD

The season for fresh, young broad/fava beans is short. They need very little preparation; just throw them into some boiling water, rinse, drain and add to pastas, risottos and salads, among other dishes. Older and frozen broad/fava beans can be used but they need a little more attention as their skins are tougher.

500 g/1 lb. shelled fresh young
   broad/fava beans or butter beans
65 ml/¼ cup olive oil
1 small red onion, finely chopped
2 garlic cloves, finely chopped
2 tablespoons freshly squeezed
   lemon juice
a small bunch of fresh dill, finely
   chopped
a handful of fresh flat-leaf parsley
   leaves
a handful of small fresh mint leaves
100 g/1 cup roughly crumbled
   feta-style cheese (see page 20),
   or storebought feta
freshly ground black pepper,
   to season

SERVES 4

Cook the broad/fava beans in a large saucepan of boiling water for 10 minutes. Rinse under cold water and drain well. (If using older broad/fava beans, slip the skins off now and discard.)

Heat 1 tablespoon of the oil in a small frying pan/skillet set over a medium heat. Add the onion and garlic and cook for 2–3 minutes, until just softened. Remove from the heat.

Put the broad/fava beans and herbs in a bowl. In a small bowl, use a fork to mix together the remaining oil and lemon juice and then pour over the salad. Stir to combine. Add the feta, stir again, and season well with black pepper before serving.

# WHEATBERRY, APPLE & PECAN SALAD

This is a twist on the a Waldorf salad with the winning combination of apple and nuts in a mayonnaise cut through with yogurt and served with wheatberries.

200 g/1 cup wheatberries
1 green apple, chopped
65 g/½ cup pecan halves
100 g/2 cups mixed salad leaves

**FOR THE YOGURT DRESSING**
50g/scant ¼ cup mayonnaise
50g/scant ¼ cup yogurt
  (see page 13), or use storebought
3 tablespoons freshly squeezed
  lemon juice
½ teaspoon salt
½ teaspoon freshly ground
  black pepper

SERVES 2–4

Put the wheatberries in a medium-sized saucepan or pot and cover completely with water by 2½ cm/1 inch. Bring to the boil over a high heat then reduce the temperature and simmer uncovered for about 50 minutes. Remove from the heat, drain and set aside.

In a large bowl, make the dressing by whisking together the mayonnaise, yogurt, lemon juice, salt and pepper. Add the apples, pecans and wheatberries and using salad tongs or a large spoon, gently fold all of the ingredients together.

Plate the salad leaves first, then add the wheatberry mix on top. Serve immediately as the apple will quickly discolour.

# FERMENTED PEARL BARLEY, MUSHROOM & WALNUT SALAD

Fermenting the barley for 5 days adds an extra flavour dimension to the grain, and a mix of seasonal mushrooms will give this salad a rich, earthy taste while the chilli adds a touch of warming spice. You'll need to start preparing the barley 4 days in advance of serving.

200 g/1 cup pearl barley
400 ml/1¾ cups vegetable stock
a handful of shelled walnut halves
1 tablespoon walnut oil
320 g/about 5 cups sliced mixed
    seasonal mushrooms
2 garlic cloves, crushed/minced
¼ teaspoon dried rosemary
¼ teaspoon dried chilli/hot red
    pepper flakes
a handful of rocket/arugula
salt and freshly ground black pepper,
    to season

**FOR THE VINAIGRETTE DRESSING**
4 spring onions/scallions,
    finely chopped
2 tablespoons walnut oil
2 teaspoons balsamic vinegar
a squeeze of fresh lemon juice
a handful of fresh flat-leaf parsley,
    finely chopped

SERVES 2–4

Place the barley in a suitable-sized sterilized container and pour 600 ml/2½ cups of cold water over the grains. Stir with a clean sterilized spoon, then cover the container with muslin. Keep in a warm place and allow to ferment for 4 days, after which time the barley will be ready to use. (It can then be stored, in the liquid, in an airtight container in the fridge for up to 5 days.)

Drain the barley, add to a large saucepan with the stock and set over medium heat. Bring to the boil and simmer for 20–30 minutes until it is tender but retains its bite.

Meanwhile, toast the walnuts in a dry frying pan/skillet set over a medium heat.

Heat the walnut oil in a separate frying pan/skillet and add the mushrooms and garlic. Fry until golden, then season with salt and pepper. Stir in the rosemary and chilli/hot red pepper flakes. Pour the mixture into a bowl and put the pan back on the stove to make the dressing.

To make the dressing, put the spring onions/scallions, walnut oil, balsamic vinegar and lemon juice in the pan and stir until well combined. Set the pan over low heat and cook until the mixture bubbles. Remove from the heat, season with salt and pepper and stir in the parsley.

To assemble the salad, put the salad leaves in a large bowl with the mushrooms and pearl barley and stir in the dressing. Toss to combine, spoon into serving bowls and serve immediately.

# SPELT, PEAR & PROSCIUTTO SALAD

Pears and Prosciutto are great vehicles for an excellent balsamic vinegar. Traditional balsamic vinegar is produced from the juice of just-harvested white grapes (typically, Trebbiano grapes) boiled down to reach a minimum sugar concentration of 30% or more in the must, which is then fermented with a slow ageing process which further concentrates the flavours. The best ones come from Modena in Italy and it's worth investing in the best quality you can find.

200 g/1 cup spelt berries
460 ml/2 cups water
a handful of fresh thyme
100 g/4 cups baby fresh spinach
    leaves, chopped
2 ripe pears, sliced
12 slices prosciutto or Parma ham
salt and freshly ground
    black pepper, to season

**FOR THE BALSAMIC DRESSING**
3½ tablespoons balsamic vinegar
6 tablespoons olive oil

SERVES 4

Soak the spelt berries in water overnight. Drain and put in a saucepan or pot. Pour in the water (making sure it's enough to cover the spelt berries). Bring to the boil over a high heat then reduce the temperature, cover and simmer for 45 minutes. Remove the lid and drain if there is any excess water. Put in a separate bowl and leave to cool.

While the spelt berries are cooling, make the dressing by whisking 2 tablespoons of the balsamic vinegar together with the olive oil.

Dress the spelt berries with the balsamic vinaigrette and sprinkle in the fresh thyme leaves. Mix in the spinach. Season with salt and pepper.

To build the salad, scatter the spelt, spinach and thyme mixture on a serving plate. Layer the sliced pears and prosciutto on top.

Drizzle the extra 1½ tablespoons of balsamic vinegar over the pears and prosciutto and serve immediately.

# BEETROOT, FIG & GRAIN SALAD
## with feta & hazelnut dressing

This substantial and delicious salad combines simple ingredients whose flavours and textures all come together effortlessly. Earthy roasted beetroot/beets, creamy goat's cheese and sweet figs, with satisfyingly chewy mixed grains and the peppery notes of rocket/arugula, all finished off with a nutty dressing. It's easy and satisfying to roast your own beetroot but this salad can also be made with unvinegared, pre-cooked ones if that's easier for you. Likewise, a 250-g/9-oz. pouch of prepared mixed grains can be substituted if you find yourself pushed for time. (See photograph on page 78.)

350 g/³⁄₄ lb. raw beetroot/beets, peeled, cut into wedges
6 garlic cloves
a few sprigs of thyme (optional)
a drizzle of olive oil
160 g/1 cup wheat berries
40 g/¼ cup black quinoa
40 g/¼ cup white quinoa
a small handful of rocket/arugula leaves from a few sprigs each of mint, flat-leaf parsley and coriander/cilantro, torn
50 g/½ cup pomegranate seeds
1 tablespoon freshly squeezed lemon juice
6 fresh figs, sliced
100 g/3½ oz. feta-style cheese (see page 20), or storebought
salt and freshly ground black pepper, to season

**FOR THE HAZELNUT DRESSING**
1 tablespoon hazelnut oil
1 tablespoon extra virgin olive oil
1 tablespoon sherry vinegar
3 tablespoons coarsely chopped toasted hazelnuts

SERVES 6

Preheat the oven to 180°C fan/200°C/400°F/Gas 6.

To make the Hazelnut Dressing, whisk together the hazelnut oil, extra virgin olive oil and sherry vinegar in a small bowl until emulsified and add the chopped hazelnuts. Season with salt and pepper and set aside.

Place the beetroot/beet wedges, garlic and sprigs of thyme on a baking sheet, coat with a little olive oil, season with salt and pepper then cover with foil. Bake in the preheated oven for about 1 hour. Once cooked, remove from the oven and leave to cool.

Using 3 different saucepans, put the wheat berries in water and boil for about 40–50 minutes until they are soft but still a little chewy, you don't want any crunch. Cook the black quinoa the same way for about 20 minutes and the white quinoa for about 12. Once all the grains are cooked, drain and lay out on a tray to cool and steam dry. Leave the quinoa naked but anoint the wheatberries with a little olive oil and season with salt and pepper whilst still warm.

Once the grains are cooled, place the rocket/arugula, herbs and pomegranate seeds on top, drizzle over a little lemon juice and tip out onto a large serving platter, mixing them together as you do. Scatter over the beetroot/beet and sliced figs, dot chunks of the goat's cheese around the dish and finish by spooning over the Hazelnut Dressing.

# SHREDDED CARROT & COURGETTE
## SALAD with sesame miso dressing

Vegetables take on a new personality when they are prepared differently. The simple act of shredding veggies finely and mixing them in a delicious dressing made with fermented miso and rice wine vinegar creates a tasty and satisfying salad.

2 carrots, grated

3 courgettes/zucchini, grated

30 g/¼ cup sesame seeds

150 g/1 cup firm tofu, chopped
(optional)

**FOR THE SESAME MISO DRESSING**

2 tablespoons red or white miso
paste

1 tablespoon rice wine vinegar

1 tablespoon sesame oil

2 tablespoons flaxseed oil

1 teaspoon finely sliced fresh ginger

2 teaspoons runny honey

SERVES 2–4

Put the carrots, courgettes/zucchini, sesame seeds and tofu in a bowl. The tofu is optional but I recommend eating this as a meal and not as a side because tofu goes so well with the miso dressing.

For the dressing, whisk all of the ingredients together to an emulsion. Pour over the mixed salad and serve.

The salad can be prepared in advance and stored in the refrigerator for up to 2 days.

# ROASTED RED PEPPER, POMEGRANATE & SUMAC RAITA

Serve this colourful, cooling yogurt-based dish with toasted pita bread, or enjoy as an accompaniment to grilled food.

2 red (bell) peppers
1 teaspoon balsamic vinegar
1 teaspoon olive oil
pinch of salt
400 g/1²/₃ cups yogurt (see page 13), or use storebought
a few tablespoons of pomegranate seeds
1 teaspoon sumac

SERVES 4–6

Grill/broil or roast the red (bell) peppers until they're charred on all sides. Wrap in a plastic bag (which makes them easier to peel afterwards), set aside to cool, then peel, de-seed and chop into short strips. Put the red (bell) pepper strips in a bowl, add the balsamic vinegar, olive oil and salt and mix together.

Fold the red (bell) pepper strips into the yogurt and stir in most of the pomegranate seeds, but set aside 1 tablespoon to garnish. Now stir in ½ teaspoon sumac.

Just before serving, garnish the raita with the reserved pomegranate seeds and sprinkle the remaining sumac over the top.

# LOADED POTATO SKINS

This is a twice-baked, but still very simple baked potato with plenty of tangy cream cheese as well as hard cheese mixed into the mashed filling, which is then returned to the oven to bake some more. You could add some hot-smoked salmon flakes or crispy bacon pieces to the mix if liked. Either way serve with a crisp green salad for a deliciously easy hot lunch.

**2 large baking potatoes**
**6 spring onions/scallions**
**150 g/scant ¾ cup cream cheese**
**(see page 16), or use storebought**
**about 80 ml/⅓ cup whole/**
**full-fat milk**
**100 g/½ cup fresh basil pesto**
**100 g/3½ oz. cheese (Parmesan,**
**Cheddar, Gouda or mozzarella)**
**rapeseed/canola oil, for baking**

SERVES 2

Preheat the oven to 220°C fan/240°C/450°F/Gas 8. Carefully stab the potatoes with a sharp knife, then rub in a little oil and salt. Place on a baking sheet and pop on the top shelf of the preheated oven. Bake for 1½ hours.

About 10 minutes before the potatoes have had their time, trim and slice the spring onions/scallions and add to a large mixing bowl with the cream cheese, milk and pesto. Grate in all of the cheese, Feel free to add any herbs, chopped olives or extra bits and bobs (such as cooked ham, bacon, tuna, other veg, etc) to the bowl if you wish. Season very well and set aside.

Remove the potatoes from the oven. Holding them with a tea/dish towel, cut in half and scoop the flesh straight into the mixing bowl. Roughly mash the ingredients together, then pile back into the skins and place back on the baking sheet. Return to the oven for 20 minutes, until golden and bubbling. Serve immediately.

# KIMCHI PANCAKE
## with black garlic crème fraîche

This take on this popular Korean dish contrasts the chewy-textured, chilli/chile hot pancake with the subtle coolness of crème fraîche, enriched with the mellow sweetness of black garlic. Kimchi is a traditional Korean fermented relish, usually made with cabbage.

100 g/³⁄₄ cup plain/all-purpose flour
¹⁄₂ teaspoon salt
100 ml/¹⁄₃ cup water
3 tablespoons kimchi liquid
(reserved from kimchi, see below)
130 g/1 cup storebought kimchi
of your choice, drained and
finely chopped
1 spring onion/scallion, finely
chopped
150 ml/²⁄₃ cup crème fraîche
(see page 46)
3 black garlic cloves, finely chopped
1 tablespoon sunflower or
vegetable oil
thinly sliced spring onion/scallion,
to garnish

SERVES 4

Make the batter by whisking together the flour, salt and water into a thick paste. Stir in the kimchi liquid, then mix in the kimchi and spring onion/scallion.

Mix together the crème fraîche and black garlic and set aside.

Heat a large frying pan/skillet until hot. Add the oil and heat well. Pour in the batter, which should sizzle as it hits the pan, spreading it to form an even layer. Fry for 3–5 minutes until set, then turn over and fry the pancake for a further 3–4 minutes until it is well browned on both sides.

Cut the kimchi pancake into portions and serve topped with the black garlic crème fraîche. Sprinkle with extra spring onions/scallions to garnish and serve.

# DUKKAH FLATBREADS with herbed labneh

500 g/3¼ cups strong white
    bread flour
1 teaspoon instant yeast
1 teaspoon sugar
1 teaspoon salt
300 ml/1¼ cups hand-hot water
2 tablespoons olive oil

**FOR THE DUKKAH**
40 g/⅓ cup shelled hazelnuts
40 g/½ cup sesame seeds
1 tablespoon ground coriander
1 tablespoon ground cumin
½ teaspoon dried chilli/hot red
    pepper flakes
salt and freshly ground black pepper

**FOR THE HERBED LABNEH**
350 g/1½ cups sheep's milk or
    cow's milk labneh (see page 14)
1 small garlic clove, crushed
3 tablespoons finely chopped fresh
    flat-leaf parsley
2 tablespoons snipped chives
1 teaspoon finely chopped fresh
    thyme leaves

SERVES 4

Dukkah, a Middle Eastern nut and spice mixture traditionally used as a dip, gives a delicious flavour and texture to these flatbreads, which contrasts nicely with the tangy labneh.

Make the batter by whisking together the flour, salt and water into a thick paste. Stir in the kimchi liquid, then mix in the kimchi and spring onion/scallion.

Mix together the crème fraîche and black garlic and set aside.

Heat a large frying pan/skillet until hot. Add the oil and heat well. Pour in the batter, which should sizzle as it hits the pan, spreading it to form an even layer. Fry for 3–5 minutes until set, then turn over and fry the pancake for a further 3–4 minutes until it is well browned on both sides.

Cut the kimchi pancake into portions and serve topped with the black garlic crème fraîche. Sprinkle with extra spring onions/scallions to garnish.

# GOAT'S CHEESE & CHARD TART

Take a shortcrust pastry case with an eggy-milky filling and load it with whatever herbs, greens, cheeses, meats (and even fish) you might have in the fridge. This recipe is a great opportunity to get inventive with gluts of seasonal greens, or clear out leftovers.

a 23-cm/9-inch shortcrust pastry
  case (either use ready-made
  pastry or follow your favourite
  recipe), baked blind
1 shallot
3 spring onions/scallions
140 g/5 oz. chard
10 g/¹/₃ oz. fresh basil
120 g/4¹/₂ oz. soft goat's cheese
2 eggs
150 ml/²/₃ cup double/heavy cream
80 ml/¹/₃ cup whole/full-fat milk
olive oil, for frying

SERVES 4–6

Preheat the oven to 180°C fan/200°C/400°F/Gas 6. Place a large baking sheet in the oven to heat up.

Quarter lengthways, peel and trim the shallots. Trim and then cut the spring onions/scallions into 6-cm/2¹/₂-inch pieces. Pull the stalks off the chard and break into several pieces, so they're not quite so long.

Add a glug of oil to a large frying pan/skillet and once hot, add the prepared onions and chard stalks. Gently fry for 15 minutes, until lightly caramelized and softening. When they've only got a couple of minutes left in the pan, add the chard leaves and let wilt with the onions and chard stalks. Once ready, remove the pan from the heat and let cool. Once cool, tear in the basil (leaves and stalks) and goat's cheese so that all the chunky fillings are in one place, ready to go.

In a jug/pitcher, whisk the eggs, double/heavy cream and milk with some seasoning.

Pile in the onion, chard and cheese mixture in the pastry case, then evenly spread it out across the base. Finally pour the egg mixture over the top.

Carefully turn to the oven for a final bake, placing it on the baking sheet on the top shelf for 30 minutes, until just set and lightly golden on top. Remove from the oven and let sit for 10 minutes before slicing and serving with a crisp green salad.

# POTATO, PEA, SPRING ONION & FETA FRITTATA

Frittatas have to be the best fridge-raid meals around. You can chuck almost anything into them and they'll do you proud. Please use the additions to the egg in these recipes as a guide and add in whatever you have to hand, even if that is just a selection of fresh green herbs.

300 g/10½ oz. Charlotte or
   new potatoes
6 eggs
2 tablespoons milk or water
3 spring onions/scallions,
   thinly sliced
80 g/²⁄₃ cup frozen peas
100 g/³⁄₄ cup feta-style cheese
   (see page 20), or use storebought
olive oil, for cooking
salt and freshly ground black pepper,
   to season

SERVES 2–4

Preheat the grill/broiler to high.

Quarter the potatoes lengthways into 2–3-cm/³⁄₄–1¹⁄₄-inch wedges, then add to a small saucepan of salted water and bring to the boil. Once boiling, cook for 5 minutes on a rapid boil. Drain and rinse under cold water.

Whisk the eggs and milk with a fork and season. Add the spring onions/scallions along with the frozen peas, and crumble in the feta.

Once the potatoes are drained, let them steam for a minute in the colander, and heat a drizzle of oil in a medium, non-stick frying pan/ skillet on a medium-high heat. Once hot, add the potatoes and fry for 5–8 minutes, tossing occasionally, until they're golden brown and tender.

Reduce the heat to low-medium and add the egg mixture to the pan. Briefl y space out the potatoes and then leave to set for 8 minutes.

Once the frittata is almost set, but there is uncooked egg in the centre, transfer to the grill/ broiler and cook for 2–3 minutes, until golden on top and set. Remove from the grill/broiler and set aside for a couple of minutes before transferring to a board and serve.

# KIMCHI CRABCAKES with sriracha mayo

This is a great dish to cook for a special summer lunch. The crabcakes are lovely served with a potato salad and some fresh rocket/arugula or fresh baby spinach drizzled in olive oil. The light, golden panko crumbs are the perfect match for the soft, sweet crabmeat and the tanginess of both the lime and kimchi cut through the crabcakes beautifully.

2 limes
85 g/3 oz. storebought kimchi of your choice, drained and finely chopped
1 large egg
115 g/1/2 cup mayonnaise
1/2 teaspoon rock salt
1/2 teaspoon freshly ground black pepper
85 g/2 cups panko breadcrumbs
225-g/8-oz. can crabmeat, drained
225 g/8 oz. king crab/jumbo crabmeat
4 tablespoons rapeseed/canola oil

**FOR THE SRIRACHA MAYO**
2 tablespoons sriracha sauce
3 tablespoons mayonnaise
2 tablespoons yogurt (see page 13), or use storebought
freshly squeezed juice of 1 lime

SERVES 6

Finely zest one of the limes then cut both of the limes into six wedges so you have 12 in total. Transfer the lime zest into a large bowl and set the wedges aside.

Add the kimchi, egg, mayonnaise, salt and pepper to the bowl with the lime zest. Using a fork, mix until well combined before adding half of the panko breadcrumbs and all of the crabmeat. Put the remaining panko breadcrumbs in a shallow dish.

Divide the crabmeat mixture into 12 equal portions and shape into little crabcake patties. Transfer the cakes to the panko dish and generously coat both sides in the breadcrumbs. Place the cakes on a baking sheet lined with baking parchment, cover lightly with clingfilm/plastic wrap and refrigerate for 30 minutes.

Heat the oil in a large frying pan/skillet over a medium heat. When the oil is hot and has started simmering, it's time to cook the crabcakes. Add the crabcakes in batches, four at a time, and cook for approx. 3 minutes per side until golden. Transfer to a cooling rack set over paper towels to drain. Repeat with the remaining crabcakes.

Serve immediately with the Sriracha Mayo and lime wedges on the side for squeezing.

# FRIED TOFU SANDWICHES with pickles

The three main components of this satisfying sandwich are: tasty bread, fried plant protein, a tasty savoury spread and freshly pickled vegetables – the combinations are endless!

240 g/8¼ oz. marinated tofu, seitan or tempeh
4 slices seeded sourdough bread
2 tablespoons Rich Miso-Tofu Dressing (see page 41), or storebought hummus
1 roasted red pepper in vinegar from a jar, sliced into strips
any tangy pickles, such as sliced gherkins or kimchi, to taste
2 handfuls of lambs' lettuce/corn salad or other salad greens
4 tablespoons seed sprouts

SERVES 2

First prepare the tofu, seitan or tempeh. Cut four 10-cm x 6-cm/ 4-inch x 2½-inch slices, 6-mm/¼-inch thick. Cook these slices by just covering the bottom of the pan with oil and fry them on both sides until browned.

Take the 4 slices of bread. First add the Rich Miso-Tofu Dressing or hummus on the bottom slices, then add 2 slices of fried tofu, seitan or tempeh, sprinkle with pickles, salad and seed sprouts and top with the remaining slices of bread.

Eat immediately, while the filling is still warm.

# REUBENS with beef, sauerkraut & Emmenthal

This is a classic American sandwich, which contains corned or salt beef, thousand island dressing, sauerkraut and melted Swiss cheese. (See photograph on page 98.)

4 tablespoons mayonnaise
3 spring onions/scallions, sliced
2 gherkins, chopped
¼ teaspoon hot horseradish sauce
a dash Worcestershire sauce
8 slices of rye bread
300 g/10½ oz. corned or salt beef, sliced
200 g/7 oz. Purple Sauerkraut (see page 38), or storebought, drained
100 g/3½ oz. Emmenthal, sliced

SERVES 4

Put the mayonnaise, spring onions, gherkins, horseradish and Worcestershire sauces in a bowl, mix well and set aside.

Preheat the grill/broiler.

Grill/broil the bread for 1–2 minutes on one side, until golden. Remove from the oven and spread dressing over the untoasted side of half the slices. Lay Emmenthal on the rest and grill/broil for 2–3 minutes just to melt.

Meanwhile, put the corned beef, then some sauerkraut over the mayonnaise-covered bread slices. Once the cheese has melted, make up the sandwiches and serve immediately.

# MAIN DISHES

# LAMB SKEWERS with za'atar labneh

Labneh, flavoured here with za'atar, a Middle Eastern herb mix, makes an excellent, tangy accompaniment to marinated lamb. Weather permitting, this would be a great dish for the barbecue. Serve it simply with flatbreads and a side salad for a taste of summer.

2 tablespoons olive oil

freshly squeezed juice of 1 lemon

2 garlic cloves, crushed

¼ teaspoon dried oregano

600 g/1¼ lbs. lamb neck fillet, cut into even-sized cubes

8 cherry tomatoes

1 red (bell) pepper, chopped into even-sized squares

1 red onion, chopped into even-sized squares

salt and freshly ground black pepper, to season

**FOR THE ZA'ATAR LABNEH**

350 g/1½ cups labneh (see page 14), or use storebought

1 tablespoon za'atar

1 tablespoon olive oil, plus extra for serving

1 tablespoon pistachio nut kernels, finely chopped

SERVES 4

First, marinate the lamb for the skewers. In a large bowl, mix together the olive oil, lemon juice, garlic and oregano and season well with salt and pepper. Add in the lamb cubes and mix until they're well coated with the marinade. Cover with clingfilm/plastic wrap and marinate in the fridge for 1–8 hours.

Take the lamb out of the fridge and bring it to room temperature before cooking. Preheat the grill/broiler to its highest setting. Thread the lamb onto skewers, alternating the meat with cherry tomatoes and sliced red pepper and onion squares. Reserve the marinade remaining in the bowl.

Place the lamb skewers on an oven tray/broiler pan and grill/broil until cooked through, around 15 minutes, turning them over halfway through cooking. Brush the meat now and then with the reserved marinade so that it stays moist.

Meanwhile, make the za'atar labneh by mixing together the labneh, za'atar and olive oil. Place the labneh in a serving bowl. Using the back of a spoon, make a shallow hollow in the centre of the labneh. Pour in a little olive oil and sprinkle over the chopped pistachios.

Serve the freshly grilled lamb skewers with the za'atar labneh on the side.

# SPINACH & CHEESE PHYLLO PIE

Burek is a baked or fried pastry from Eastern Europe, often surrounding a cheese and vegetable filling. Traditionally, it is enjoyed with a glass of milk kefir (see page 24), which further increases your intake of fermented foods.

300 g/10 oz. fresh spinach
(or 420 g/ 14 oz. frozen spinach, defrosted and drained)
110 g/½ cup cottage cheese (see page 18), or use storebought
100 g/scant ½ cup yogurt
(see page 13), or use storebought
1 egg, beaten
2 tablespoons olive oil, plus extra to brush
2 tablespoons sparkling water
½ teaspoon bicarbonate of soda/baking soda
1 teaspoon salt
250 g/8 oz. large filo/phyllo sheets
18-cm/7-in. square baking pan
(4 cm/1¾ in. deep), greased

MAKES 4–6 SERVINGS

Preheat the oven to 160°C fan/180°C/350°F/gas 4.

Blanch the spinach in a saucepan of boiling water for 30 seconds. Drain and squeeze to get rid of excess water. Chop finely, then put in a mixing bowl with the cottage cheese, yogurt, egg, oil, water, bicarbonate of soda/baking soda and salt and mix well.

Lay a filo/phyllo sheet in the base of the baking pan, leaving the excess pastry hanging over one side of the pan. Brush with oil. Lay another sheet on top so that the overhang is on the opposite side of the pan. Spread a generous tablespoon of spinach mixture over the filo/phyllo sheet. Lay another 2 sheets over the filling and scrunch up the excess pastry to fit the pan. Brush with oil. Spread another generous tablespoon of spinach mixture over the filo/phyllo sheet. Lay another 2 sheets over the filling and scrunch up the excess pastry to fit the pan. Brush with oil. Keep going until all the spinach mixture is used up. You should end with a layer of filling.

Finally, fold over the overhanging pastry to cover the top of the burek and brush all over with more oil. If the top isn't entirely covered with pastry, add another sheet and brush with oil.

Bake in the preheated oven for 40 minutes until deep golden and risen. Remove from the oven and leave to cool for a few minutes before serving.

# ROASTED ONION, TOMATO & CHICKPEA CURRY with cucumber raita

This is a great curry to make when you want something wholesome, packed with vegetables, goodness and flavour.

1 garlic bulb
2 red onions, skin on,
   cut into wedges
1 tablespoon coriander seeds
1 tablespoon mustard seeds
1 tablespoon ground turmeric
1 tablespoon ground ginger
1 cinnamon stick
2 tablespoons medium curry powder
1 onion, thinly sliced
1 carrot, finely chopped
1 celery stick/stalk, finely chopped
1 sweet potato, chopped into
   2–3-cm/³⁄₄–1¹⁄₄-in. chunks
600 g/21 oz. mixed fresh tomatoes,
   roughly chopped
100 ml/¹⁄₃ cup plus 1 tablespoon
   boiling water
1 vegetable stock cube
2 x 400-g/14-oz. cans chickpeas
200 g/7 oz. spinach
salt and freshly ground black pepper
vegetable oil, for roasting
basmati rice and canned lentils,
   to serve

**FOR THE CUCUMBER RAITA**
¹⁄₂ cucumber (approx. 160 g/5³⁄₄ oz.)
130 ml/¹⁄₂ cup yogurt (see page 13),
   or use storebought
grated zest and juice of 1 lime
1 garlic clove, peeled

SERVES 4

Preheat the oven to 200°C fan/220°C/425°F/Gas 7.

Break up the garlic bulb and put onto a baking sheet with the onion wedges. Drizzle with vegetable oil, season and toss to coat. Roast in the preheated oven for 25 minutes, until roasted and coloured.

Meanwhile, roughly crush the coriander seeds in a pestle and mortar. Heat a small frying pan/skillet over a medium heat, add the mustard seeds and crushed coriander seeds to the pan and toast for a couple of minutes, until fragrant. Remove from the heat and transfer to a small bowl. Add the remaining spices.

Heat a glug of vegetable oil in a large saucepan or casserole over a medium heat and, once hot, add the onion. Fry for 10 minutes until tender and starting to lightly caramelize. Add the carrot, celery and sweet potato to the pan along with the spices. Cook for 5 minutes, stirring often.

Once the red onions and garlic are ready, remove from the oven. Tear away the onion skins, and pull the garlic flesh from their skins too. Briefly mash the garlic flesh. Add the roasted onions and garlic to the curry.

Next, add the tomatoes, boiling water, stock cube, chickpeas and chickpea water from the cans to the pan and bring to the boil. Reduce the heat and simmer for 45 minutes, stirring often.

To make the raita, grate the cucumber into a bowl, then add the yogurt and lime zest and juice, grate in the garlic clove and add a pinch of seasoning to the bowl. Mix well to combine and season to taste.

When the curry is a couple of minutes away from being ready, add the spinach and mix well to submerge and let wilt. Taste the curry, season generously and taste again.

Serve with cooked hot rice, lentils and the cucumber raita.

# RICOTTA & SPINACH DUMPLINGS
## with cherry tomato sauce

Inspired by Italian cuisine, this recipe uses ricotta, together with spinach, to make little dumplings. The sauce here is a tomato one, flavoured with basil, lemon and chilli/chile.

400 g/14 oz. fresh spinach

250 g/1 cup ricotta (see page 15), or use storebought

2 eggs

100 g/¾ cup fine semolina, plus extra for coating

50 g/⅔ cup grated Parmesan, plus extra for serving

freshly grated nutmeg

butter, for greasing

salt and freshly ground black pepper

**FOR THE CHERRY TOMATO SAUCE**

2 tablespoons olive oil

2 garlic cloves, chopped

a splash of dry white wine (optional)

2 x 395-g/14-oz. cans of peeled cherry tomatoes

2 pinches of dried chilli/hot red pepper flakes

a generous handful of fresh basil leaves

a sprinkle of freshly grated lemon zest

SERVES 4

Rinse the spinach well, discarding any discoloured or wilted leaves. Place it in a large, heavy-based saucepan and cook, covered, over medium heat until the spinach has just wilted, so that it retains some texture. Strain in a colander, pressing out any excess moisture and set it aside to cool. Once cooled, chop the spinach finely, again squeezing out any excess moisture.

While the spinach is cooling, place the ricotta in a clean tea/dish towel in a sieve/strainer over a bowl to drain off any excess moisture.

For the tomato sauce, heat the olive oil in a heavy-based frying pan. Add the garlic and fry, stirring, until golden brown. Add the wine and cook, stirring, until it has largely evaporated. Add the cherry tomatoes, chilli/hot red pepper flakes and lemon zest. Tear the basil (reserving a few leaves) and mix in. Season with salt and pepper. Cook, uncovered, for 5–10 minutes, stirring now and then until the sauce has thickened.

Place the ricotta in a large bowl and break it up with a fork. Mix in the finely chopped spinach thoroughly. Add the eggs, semolina and Parmesan and mix well. Season with salt, pepper and nutmeg and mix again.

Sprinkle semolina on a large plate. Take a teaspoon of ricotta mixture and, using a second teaspoon, shape it into a nugget. Using teaspoons, place this ricotta dumpling on the semolina and roll, lightly coating it. Repeat the process until all the ricotta has been shaped into dumplings.

Preheat the oven to 190°C (350°F) Gas 5. Gently reheat the tomato sauce. Generously butter a heatproof serving dish and place it in the oven to warm through. Line a plate with paper towels.

Bring a large saucepan of salted water to the boil. Cook the dumplings in batches – you shouldn't over-crowd the pan. Cook over medium heat until they float to the surface, around 2–3 minutes. Remove the dumplings using a shallow, slotted spoon, drain on the paper-lined plate, then carefully transfer to the serving dish in the oven to keep warm. Repeat the process until all the dumplings have been cooked.

Tear the remaining basil leaves and stir into the cherry tomato sauce. Serve the dumplings with the sauce and extra Parmesan on the side.

# MISO-MARINATED COD FILLETS

To ensure the fish is flavoursome and really melts in the mouth, marinate it for 2–3 days before cooking. This recipe is a great option for entertaining as, apart from being utterly delicious and guaranteed to impress, you can prep it in advance. If liked, you can serve it with some Pickled Ginger (see page 35) as a condiment.

4 x 200-g/7-oz. black cod fillets, or sablefish (Chilean sea bass and salmon also work well)
235 ml/1 cup sake
235 ml/1 cup mirin
250 g/1 cup white miso paste
150 g/¾ cup caster/white granulated sugar
1 tablespoon Japanese furikake seasoning
25 g/⅓ cup spring onions/scallions, finely sliced
Pickled Ginger, to serve (see page 35)

SERVES 4

Rinse the fish fillets. Gently but thoroughly pat dry with paper towels. Set aside.

Place the sake and mirin in a heavy-based pan and bring to the boil over a high heat. Boil for a few minutes to cook off the alcohol, then simmer for 10 minutes.

Whisk in the miso paste until fully dissolved. Add the sugar, stirring continuously to make sure it doesn't stick to the bottom of the pan and burn. Simmer over a low heat for about 45 minutes, stirring occasionally. The marinade will thicken slightly and caramelize. Set aside to cool to room temperature.

Once the marinade has cooled completely, put three-quarters intoa non-metallic, sealable storage container or ziplock bag. Add the fish, ensuring it is completely coated in the marinade. Refrigerate for 2–3 days, stirring occasionally to ensure the fish is well marinated. Reserve the remaining marinade in the fridge to use later – some for cooking and some for serving.

Preheat the oven to 160°C fan/180°C/350°F/gas 4.

Remove the fish from the marinade, but leave a good coating on the fish. Lay the fish on a baking sheet and bake in the preheated oven for about 10 minutes.

Preheat the grill/broiler to medium-high. Pour a little of the reserved marinade over each baked fish fillet and grill/broil for 3–5 minutes, or until golden brown and caramelized.

Drizzle any remaining marinade over the fish, sprinkle with furikake, and top with sliced spring onions/scallions. Serve immediately with steamed greens and rice and Pickled Ginger.

**TIP** You can also use this marinade recipe with chicken, just cook it for a little longer in the oven, ensuring the meat is cooked through before you put it under the grill/broiler.

# SPAGHETTI with Gorgonzola, pecan & mascarpone sauce

The toasted pecan nuts add texture to this rich and creamy cheese sauce. Gorgonzola is a strongly flavoured blue cheese that is perfect combined with the milder mascarpone. Other blue cheeses you could use are Roquefort or even Stilton.

4.5 litres/4¾ quarts water
450 g/1 lb. dried spaghetti
25 g/2 tablespoons unsalted butter
1 garlic clove, peeled and crushed
175 g/6 oz. Gorgonzola, crumbled
175 g/¾ cup mascarpone
   (see page 19), or use storebought
a pinch of ground mace or freshly
   grated nutmeg
100 g/⅔ cup pecan nuts, toasted
   and roughly chopped
2 tablespoons snipped chives
salt and freshly ground black pepper,
   to season

SERVES 4

In a large saucepan over a high heat, bring the water to the boil and add 2 teaspoons of salt. Add the dried spaghetti, allow the water to return to the boil before turning the heat down to medium. Cook the spaghetti for 10 minutes if you like it al dente and a couple of minutes longer if you like it softer.

Meanwhile, melt the butter in a saucepan and gently fry the garlic over low heat for 2–3 minutes, or until soft but not browned. Stir in the Gorgonzola, mascarpone, mace or nutmeg along with the salt and pepper. Cook gently until the sauce is heated through but the cheese still has a little texture.

Remove the pan from the heat and stir in the pecan nuts and chives. Season to taste, then add the cooked spaghetti and mix thoroughly. Serve immediately.

# ORZO & ROAST COURGETTE
## with semi-dried tomato dressing

If the thought of pasta salad makes you recoil with images of cold pasta mixed with canned corn, drowned in mayo, fear not – this fresh, vibrant salad bears no resemblance.

**250 g/4 cups orzo pasta**

**2 courgettes/zucchini, cut in half lengthways**

**70 g/²/₃ cup feta-style cheese (see page 20), or use storebought**

**70 g/²/₃ cup pitted black olives, halved**

**20 g/scant ½ cup flat-leaf parsley leaves, chopped**

**salt and freshly ground black pepper, to season**

**FOR THE SEMI-DRIED TOMATO DRESSING**

**1 garlic bulb**

**125 ml/½ cup olive oil, plus 2 teaspoons for roasting**

**80 g/³/₄ cup semi-dried tomatoes in oil, drained**

**¼ teaspoon caster/granulated sugar**

**1 tablespoon balsamic vinegar**

SERVES 6

Preheat the oven to 180°C fan/200°C /400°F/gas 6.

Begin by making the dressing. Cut the top part off the top of the garlic head to expose the individual garlic cloves. Place the garlic head, cut-side down, onto a square piece of foil and drizzle with 2 teaspoons of olive oil. Lift the foil up around the garlic and place on a baking sheet. Roast in the preheated oven for 45 minutes. Remove from the oven, open the foil wrap and set aside to cool. When the garlic is cool enough to handle, squeeze the cloves out of the skin, coarsely chop the garlic flesh and discard the skin.

Reduce the oven temperature to 160°C fan/180°C/350°F/gas 4.

Place 50 g/½ cup of the semi-dried tomatoes in a food processor with the remaining olive oil, sugar, vinegar, salt and pepper. Blend and pour into a large mixing bowl.

Roughly chop the remaining semi-dried tomatoes and stir through the oil mixture with the roasted garlic.

To prepare the orzo pasta, place it in a saucepan or pot of salted boiling water set over a medium heat. Bring to the boil and cook for about 8 minutes until al dente. Drain well before transferring to the bowl with the dressing while still warm. Toss to coat the orzo.

Preheat a griddle/grill-pan over a medium heat and, when hot, char the courgettes/zucchinis, flesh-side down for 2 minutes until marked. Transfer the courgettes/zucchinis skin-side down to a baking sheet, season with salt and pepper and cook in the still-warm oven for 10 minutes. Remove from the oven and cut on the diagonal at 2-cm/³/₄-inch intervals.

Add the courgettes/zucchinis, feta, olives and parsley and stir. Add a final drizzle of olive oil and serve.

# BUTTERNUT SQUASH & CHICORY PASTA BAKE

A twist on a traditional lasagne, this pasta bake is a lovely, wholesome veggie alternative that equally hits the spot. You could try it with plenty of roasted veg, but a sweet root vegetable such as butternut squash seems to work best.

800–900 g/1¾–2 lb. butternut squash, unpeeled

50 g/3½ tablespoons butter

50 g/6 tablespoons plain/all-purpose flour

650 ml/2¾ cups whole/full-fat milk

40 g/½ cup grated Parmesan, plus extra to top

2 chicory heads

8–10 dried lasagne sheets

250 g/1¼ cups ricotta cheese (see page 15), or use storebought

a generous handful of fresh basil leaves

salt and freshly ground pepper, to season

SERVES 6

Preheat the oven to 200°C fan/220°C/425°F/Gas 7.

Trim, then chop the butternut squash into 2–3-cm/¾–1¼-inch chunks (no need to peel). Add to a large baking sheet, season well, drizzle with a glug of olive oil and toss to coat. Place on the top shelf of the oven and roast for 35 minutes until tender and lightly caramelized.

Melt the butter in a medium saucepan set over a medium heat and once sizzling, add the flour. Mix very well and cook for a couple minutes. Next, add a splash of milk which will turn the roux firmer. Allow the milk to be absorbed before you add another generous splash. Continue this process until all the milk is used. Let the sauce cook and thicken for about 5 minutes, stirring constantly – it should end up with a custard-like thickness. Remove from the heat, add the Parmesan, stir to combine, then season very well (make sure you taste it).

Separate the chicory leaves, then cut them in half lengthways. Scatter a layer of squash on the base of a baking dish, followed by chicory, some dollops of ricotta randomly placed, then a layer of lasagne sheets. Top with the white sauce and a scattering of basil leaves (and their stalks, torn). Repeat the layers (starting with the roasted squash), continuing until you've used up all of the ingredients. Finish with a very generous scattering of basil leaves on the final layer of béchamel and an extra sprinkle of seasoning and Parmesan, too. Place on the middle shelf of the preheated oven and bake for 40 minutes, until tender, golden brown on top and bubbling happily.

Serve with peas or a fresh, crunchy salad.

# HONEY, MISO & SOY AUBERGINE,
## with yogurt & coriander

The key to this delicious dish is cooking the aubergines/eggplants for a long time, until you achieve a deep caramelization. (See photograph on page 100.)

4 aubergines/eggplants

4 tablespoons runny honey

100 g/6 tablespoons red miso paste

3 tablespoons soy sauce

3 tablespoons vegetable oil

300 g/1¹/₃ cups yogurt (see page 13),
   or use storebought

30 g/1 oz. freshly chopped
   coriander/cilantro

1 fresh red chilli/chile, thinly sliced

30 g/1 oz. crispy onions

1 teaspoon pul biber pepper flakes,
   or similar

salt and freshly ground
   black pepper, to season

*large baking sheet lined with
   parchment paper*

SERVES 4-6

Preheat the oven to 180°C fan/200°C/400°F/gas 6.

Quarter the aubergines/eggplants lengthways and put onto the prepared baking sheet. Add the honey, miso paste, soy sauce and vegetable oil to a bowl with some black pepper and mix with a fork to combine, then pour liberally over the aubergines/eggplants and rub into the wedges with your hands.

Place the dressed aubergines/eggplants on the top shelf of the preheated oven and bake for 1 hour, turning and basting 3 times. If the aubergines/eggplants colour too much, cover with an upside-down baking sheet.

Meanwhile, season the yogurt with a pinch of salt and pepper and spread over a large serving dish.

Once the aubergines/eggplants are very soft, sticky and well-coloured, transfer to the serving dish in a pile on top of the yogurt, top with the coriander/cilantro, crispy onions and fresh chilli/chile, finishing with the pul biber pepper flakes. Spoon over any remaining roasting sauce onto the dish and serve.

# ROASTED RADICCHIO with blue cheese dressing

Radicchio has a striking red and white colour and natural bitterness that, when roasted, mellows to a warm smokiness. A tangy blue cheese dressing, crunchy walnuts and seeds and a drizzle of pomengrate molasses make it rather special. (See photograph on page 120.)

100 g/½ cup pearled spelt

2 medium radicchio heads

a splash of olive oil

2 tablespoons butter, melted

1 tablespoon runny honey

4 walnuts halves, crumbled

1 tablespoon toasted pumpkin
    seeds/pepitas

2 tablespoons pomegranate
    molasses

salt and freshly ground black pepper,
    to season

**FOR THE BLUE CHEESE DRESSING**

50 g/2 oz. any blue cheese

3 tablespoons yogurt (see page 13),
    or use storebought

2 tablespoons extra virgin olive oil

a few squeezes of fresh lemon juice

a pinch of finely chopped fresh
    flat-leaf parsley

a pinch of salt

SERVES 4–6

Preheat the oven to 200°C fan/220°C/425°F/gas 7.

Rinse the pearled spelt under running water. Tip into a large saucepan and cover with salted water. Simmer for about 20–30 minutes, or until cooked; it should be chewy but without any crunch. Drain, season and set aside.

Trim the radicchio and quarter lengthways (or cut into sixths if they are on the large side) and put them on a baking sheet. Drizzle with a little olive oil, the melted butter and just a smidge of honey and season with salt and pepper. Toss with your hands to coat evenly. Roast in the preheated oven for about 15–20 minutes, turning them once during cooking. They are done when the stalk is just knife tender. Pour the cooked spelt into the baking sheet to coat in any of the juices, then transfer everything to a serving dish or platter.

To make the Blue Cheese Dressing, simply mash all the ingredients together with a fork in a small bowl and add a splash of water if it needs loosening to a pouring consistency. Drizzle the dressing over the radicchio and spelt, sprinkle with crumbled walnuts and pumpkin seeds and finish with a drizzle with pomegranate molasses.

# TOFU NOODLES with mushrooms & marmite

It may sound weird to add Marmite/yeast extract to noodles and tofu, but honestly, it's really delicious and not overpowering. Marmite adds some umami (or savoury) depth without any effort at all. Even if you don't like Marmite, you will still enjoy this recipe.

3 garlic cloves
30-g/1-oz. piece of fresh ginger
1 fresh red chilli/chile
200 g/7 oz. mushrooms
225 g/8 oz. smoked tofu
100 g/3½ oz. greens
2 tablespoons sesame oil
1 tablespoon Marmite/yeast extract
1 tablespoon rice vinegar
300 g/10½ oz. udon noodles
1 lime, cut into wedges
rapeseed/canola oil, for frying
salt and freshly ground pepper,
   to season

SERVES 2

Peel and thinly slice the garlic. Trim, then cut the ginger into matchsticks. Trim, then thinly slice the chilli/chile. Thickly slice the mushrooms. Cut the tofu into 2-cm/¾-inch cubes. Slice the greens into long, slim pieces; halve any purple sprouting broccoli (lengthways too if they're quite thick), thickly slice any leafy greens, leave spinach or kale whole, cut pak choi into thirds.

Add a glug of oil to large frying pan/skillet set over a medium-high heat and once hot, add the tofu cubes and fry them for about 10 minutes until golden on all sides, turning often. Transfer the golden tofu to a plate.

Pile the garlic, ginger, chilli/chile and mushrooms into the pan. Fry for 5 minutes until softening and slightly browned. Add the greens and toss to combine, letting them wilt and briefly cook for 2 minutes. Return the tofu to the pan and add the sesame oil, Marmite/yeast extract and vinegar. Stir to mix all the ingredients together, then push them to the sides of the pan to create a gap in the centre. Tip the noodles into the gap so they have direct contact with the base of the pan. Leave for 30 seconds, then start to jiggle them a bit to help them loosen up. Toss all the ingredients together for a couple of minutes until piping hot and fully combined. Finish with a good squeeze of lime juice, season and remove from the heat. Serve immediately.

# SAFFRON SHRIMP with fermented barley pilaf

Like rice, there are many forms of barley. Hull-less barley has most of its outer layer intact so it is considered a wholegrain. The bran layer contains the fibre, vitamins and protein. It is chewy and mild tasting so it is very versatile. It's great in soups, salads and pilafs. See page 73 for instructions on how to ferment the barley before using it in this recipe.

1 onion, chopped

2 tablespoons plus 1 teaspoon vegetable oil

1 garlic clove, crushed

200 g/1 cup fermented pearl barley (see page 73)

480 ml/2 cups vegetable stock

1 bay leaf

12 medium raw prawns/shrimp, peeled and deveined

1 teaspoon paprika

1 teaspoon turmeric

1 teaspoon ground cinnamon

1 teaspoon ground cardamom

a pinch of saffron threads

a few sprigs of fresh flat-leaf parsley, to garnish

SERVES 2

In a medium saucepan or pot, fry the onion in 2 tablespoons of vegetable oil for 4–5 minutes over high heat. Reduce the heat, then add the garlic and barley, toasting for 3 minutes. Then add 240 ml/ 1 cup water, the stock and bay leaf. Bring to the boil, then cover and simmer for about 30-40 minutes. The grains will be softened and chewy when fully cooked.

In a separate medium non-stick frying pan/skillet, heat 1 teaspoon of vegetable oil over a medium heat and add the paprika, turmeric, cinnamon, cardamom and saffron. Add the prawns/shrimp and fry for 3 minutes on each side, or until they are completely opaque.

Remove the bay leaf from the barley and scoop a generous amount and 6 prawns/shrimp on each plate. Garnish with fresh flat-leaf parsley.

# DESSERTS
# & BAKES

# BUTTERMILK PANNA COTTA
## with cloudberry coulis

Using buttermilk in panna cotta gives it a lovely, subtle flavour. The ivory-coloured panna cotta together with the orange cloudberry or mango makes a very pretty, elegant dessert.

**8 g/approx. 4 sheets leaf gelatine**

**300 ml/1¼ cups double/ heavy cream**

**75 g/⅓ cup vanilla sugar or caster/white granulated sugar**

**300 ml/1¼ cups buttermilk (see page 10), or use storebought**

**1 teaspoon vanilla bean paste for the coulis**

**6 tablespoons cloudberry jam (if cloudberry jam is hard to find, use 200 ml/6½ oz. canned Alphonso mango pulp instead)**

**1 tablespoon freshly squeezed orange juice**

*6 ramekins or similar small serving bowls*

MAKES 6

Soak the leaf gelatine in cold water for 5 minutes, then squeeze dry.

In a small pan, gently heat together the double/heavy cream and sugar, stirring until the sugar has dissolved. If using caster/granulated sugar rather than vanilla sugar, add a little more vanilla bean paste later when stirring in the buttermilk.

Remove from direct heat, add in the soaked gelatine and stir in well, until the gelatine has dissolved.

Transfer to a bowl and stir in the buttermilk and vanilla paste, mixing together well.

Divide the buttermilk mixture among 6 ramekins or small serving bowls. Cool, cover and chill until it has set, around 3 hours.

To serve, mix together the cloudberry jam and orange juice. Spoon a little of the cloudberry coulis over the top of each panna cotta and serve. Alternatively, dip the bowls briefly in hot water, carefully turn out the panna cottas onto serving plates and spoon over the cloudberry coulis and serve.

# SAFFRON & CARDAMOM
# LABNEH with mango

This rich and fragrant dessert is an exotic, pleasantly indulgent
way in which to round off any meal.

2 pinches of saffron strands

2 green cardamom pods

350 g/1½ cups cow's milk labneh
(see page 14), or use storebought

3 tablespoons icing/confectioners'
sugar, sifted

2 medium mangoes, peeled
and sliced

1 tablespoon finely ground
pistachio kernels

SERVES 4

Finely grind the saffron. Mix with 1 teaspoon of freshly boiled water
and set aside to infuse for 15 minutes.

Crack the green cardamom pods and remove and finely grind
the black seeds with a pestle and mortar, discarding the husks.

Fold together the labneh, icing/confectioners' sugar, cooled
saffron water and ground cardamom, mixing in well. Cover with
clingfilm/plastic wrap and chill.

To serve, divide the mangoes among 4 serving bowls. Top with
saffron labneh, sprinkle with the ground pistachio kernels and serve.

# COEUR À LA CRÈME
## with strawberries & passion fruit

This classic French dish makes an elegant dessert, though do bear in mind that ideally you should start preparing it the day before you plan to serve it. Combining it with fresh fruit, such as strawberries and passion fruit or with apricot compote and raspberries, helps to offset the richness.

**200 g/1 cup cream cheese (see page 16), or use storebought**
**150 ml/²/₃ cups double/heavy cream**
**1 tablespoon vanilla sugar or caster/white granulated sugar**
**½ teaspoon vanilla bean paste (optional)**
**4 ripe passion fruits, halved**
**200 g/1 pint fresh strawberries, hulled and halved**

*4 heart-shaped coeur à la crème moulds/molds*
*4 muslin/cheesecloth squares*

SERVES 4

Line 4 heart-shaped coeur à la crème moulds/molds with 4 muslin/cheesecloth squares.

In a large bowl, use a balloon whisk to gently whisk together the cream cheese, double/heavy cream, sugar and vanilla bean paste until thoroughly folded together.

Divide the cream cheese mixture evenly among the 4 lined moulds/molds. Gently fold the muslin/ cheesecloth over the filling, covering it completely.

Place the moulds/molds in a baking pan or a deep dish and set aside for at least 8 hours in the refrigerator.

To serve, carefully remove each cream cheese heart from its mould/mold and onto serving plates. Spoon some passion fruit pulp around each heart and decorate each plate with some strawberries before serving.

# RHUBARB & MASCARPONE TART

The pleasing sharpness of rhubarb contrasts wonderfully well
with the creamy mascarpone filling in this delicious tart.

**FOR THE FILLING**
500 g/1 lb. fresh rhubarb, cut into
    2-cm/1-in. slices
175 g/³/₄ cup caster/white
    granulated sugar
30 g/2 tablespoons salted butter,
    softened
225 g/scant 1 cup mascarpone
    (see page 19), or use storebought
30 g/¹/₄ cup plain/all-purpose flour
finely grated zest of 1 orange
2 eggs, separated
100 ml/scant ¹/₂ cup double/
    heavy cream

**FOR THE SHORTBREAD BASE**
135 g/9 tablespoons salted butter,
    softened
65 g/¹/₃ cup caster/granulated sugar
160 g/1¹/₄ cups plain/all-purpose
    flour
15 g/2 tablespoons cornflour/
    cornstarch
25 g/3 tablespoons rice flour

**FOR THE SYRUP**
2 teaspoons arrowroot
freshly squeezed juice of 1 orange
*23-cm/9-in. loose-based tart pan*
*baking parchment*
*baking beans*

SERVES 8-10

Preheat the oven to 180°C fan/190°C/375°F/gas 5. Put the rhubarb
for the filling in an ovenproof dish, sprinkle 60 g/¹/₃ cup of the sugar
over the top and cover with foil. Roast in the preheated oven for about
15 minutes. Remove the dish from the oven and strain the rhubarb,
reserving the juice for later. Set aside. Leave the oven on.

To make the shortbread base, put all the ingredients in a large bowl
and rub together using your fingertips until it forms a paste. Knead
gently into a smooth ball of dough. Alternatively, put the ingredients
in the bowl of a food processor or electric stand mixer and blend until
it forms a smooth ball of dough. Roll out the pastry on a lightly floured
work surface to form a circle about 5 cm/2 inches larger than the pan.
Drape the pastry over the rolling pin and transfer it to the tart pan.
Gently mould the pastry into the base and sides. Trim the top edge with
a sharp knife. Line the tart case with a sheet of baking parchment. Fill
it with baking beans and blind bake for 15–20 minutes. Remove from
the oven, remove the baking parchment and beans.

To make the filling, put the butter, remaining sugar, mascarpone,
flour and orange zest into a large bowl. Beat until evenly mixed, then
add the egg yolks and cream. Beat to a creamy consistency and set aside.

Put the egg whites in a grease-free bowl and whisk on high speed
until light and foamy and soft peaks are formed. Transfer to the
mascarpone mixture and whisk together, then spoon into the tart case.
Distribute the rhubarb evenly over the filling. Bake for 40–45 minutes
or until golden-brown and the filling is set like a hot soufflé – firm but
with a slight wobble!

To make the syrup, stir together the arrowroot and 2 tablespoons
water in a cup. Put the reserved rhubarb juice and the orange juice
into a saucepan and bring to the boil. Remove from the heat and start
stirring in the arrowroot – it may not all be needed, depending on how
much juice you've produced from your rhubarb. The syrup should be
just slightly thickened, as it thickens further with cooling.

Serve the tart warm with the syrup poured on top.

# SOUR CREAM RAISIN PIE

This is almost like a very light cheesecake baked in a double crust – very rich and luscious. Serve it with extra whole raisins plumped up in sweetened rum overnight. This is always best served cold as it will be too soft to cut if warm.

**FOR THE PIE CRUST**

375 g/3 cups plain/all-purpose flour

a good pinch of salt

250 g/1 cup plus 2 tablespoons white cooking fat/shortening, chilled and diced

1 egg, beaten

1 tablespoon white wine vinegar

4 tablespoons ice-cold water

**FOR THE PIE FILLING**

150 g/1 cup large juicy raisins, chopped

3 tablespoons spiced rum

2 large eggs

225 g/1 cup plus 2 tablespoons caster/granulated sugar

250 ml/1 cup sour cream (see page 11), or use storebought

1 tablespoon freshly squeezed lemon juice

¼ teaspoon freshly grated nutmeg

2–3 tablespoons demerara/raw brown sugar, for dredging

*23-cm/9-in. metal pie plate*

*baking sheet lined with parchment paper*

SERVES 4-6

Preheat the oven to 220°C fan/230°C/450°F/gas 8 and set a heavy baking sheet on the middle shelf. Soak the chopped raisins in the rum for an hour until the rum is absorbed.

Sift the flour and salt into a large mixing bowl and cut in the fat with two round-bladed knives until thoroughly combined. (You can also do this in a food processor.) In a separate bowl, mix together the beaten egg, vinegar and water. Pour this wet mixture into the dry mixture and cut it in with the knives again.

Tip out onto a lightly floured surface and knead lightly until smooth, then shape into a flattened ball. Wrap in clingfilm/plastic wrap and chill for at least 30 minutes.

Divide the pastry dough into 2 pieces. Roll one half out on a lightly floured surface and use it to line the pie plate. Trim off the excess pastry.

Use an electric hand whisk to whisk the eggs with the caster/granulated sugar until the mixture is pale and mousse-like. Set aside.

Reserve 2 tablespoons of the sour cream for the glaze. Whip the remaining sour cream with the lemon juice, nutmeg and salt until slightly thickened. Carefully fold into the egg mixture, then fold in the soaked chopped raisins. Spoon into the pie crust.

Roll out the remaining pastry thinly so that it will cover the top of the pie. Brush the edges of the pie with a little water, pick up the pastry on the rolling pin and lift it over the pie to cover it. Fold the top crust carefully under the lower crust and press the edges together to seal.

Brush with the reserved sour cream and dredge with the demerara/raw brown sugar. Slash the top a couple of times to allow the steam to escape. Place the pie on the baking sheet in the preheated oven and bake for 10 minutes. Reduce the oven temperature to 160°C fan/180°C/350°F/gas 4 and bake for a further 20 minutes until the crust is set and pale coloured. Leave to cool before serving.

# CARROT CAKE
## with mascarpone & lemon frosting

Moist with a pleasant sweetness, there's something honest and wholesome about freshly-baked carrot cake with a fluffy mascarpone topping.

150 g/³⁄₄ cup packed light brown soft sugar
1 egg
170 ml/³⁄₄ cup corn oil
140 g/1 cup plus 1¹⁄₂ tablespoons wholemeal/whole-wheat flour
¹⁄₂ teaspoon baking powder
1 teaspoon ground cinnamon
¹⁄₂ teaspoon freshly grated nutmeg
¹⁄₄ teaspoon salt
1 ripe banana, mashed
50 g/¹⁄₃ cup chopped walnuts
30 g/3 tablespoons sultanas/ golden raisins
125 g/²⁄₃ cup grated carrots

**FOR THE MASCARPONE TOPPING**
100 g/scant ¹⁄₂ cup mascarpone (see page 19), or use storebought
40 g/¹⁄₃ cup icing/confectioners' sugar
10 g/2 teaspoons salted butter, softened
a squeeze of lemon juice (optional)
grated lemon zest, to garnish
*500-g/1-lb. loaf pan lined with a paper loaf-pan liner*

SERVES 8

Preheat the oven to 160°C fan/170°C/325°F/gas 3.

Put the sugar, egg and corn oil in a large bowl and lightly beat together. Add the flour, baking powder, cinnamon, nutmeg and salt and stir to a smooth mixture. Add the mashed banana, walnuts and sultanas/golden raisins, followed by the carrot, and stir together.

Spoon the mixture into the prepared loaf pan and bake in the preheated oven for 55 minutes. A skewer inserted into the middle of the cake should come out clean. Remove from the oven and allow to cool in the pan for about 15 minutes, then turn out onto a wire rack to cool completely.

To make the topping, put the mascarpone, icing/confectioners' sugar and butter into a bowl and whisk until light and creamy. If desired, add a squeeze of lemon or lime juice to bring a bit of zing to the frosting. Spread the topping over the cake and garnish with lemon zest. Cut into slices to serve.

# ORANGE SYRUP SEMOLINA CAKE
## with crème fraîche

This soft, buttery cake contrasts nicely with the tangy crème fraîche on the side and makes an excellent dessert. (See photograph on page 126.)

**FOR THE CAKE**

150 g/10 tablespoons butter, softened

175 g/¾ cup plus 2 tablespoons caster/granulated sugar

grated zest and freshly squeezed juice of ½ orange

2 eggs

100 ml/6 tablespoons crème fraîche (see page 12), or use storebought, plus extra to serve

125 g/1 cup plain/all-purpose flour, sifted

1 teaspoon baking powder

125 g/1 cup plus 2 tablespoons fine semolina

a pinch of salt

**FOR THE ORANGE SYRUP**

freshly squeezed juice of 1 large orange

150 g/¾ cup caster/granulated sugar

1 teaspoon orange blossom extract

*loose-based 20 cm/8 in. cake pan*

SERVES 8

Preheat the oven to 160°C fan/180°C/350°F/gas 4.

In a mixing bowl, cream together the butter and sugar until well-mixed. Add the orange zest and juice, then the eggs, one at a time, followed by the crème fraîche and mix well. Add the flour, baking power, semolina and salt and fold in. Transfer to the cake pan and bake in the preheated oven for 1 hour until golden-brown.

While the cake is baking, prepare the orange syrup. Place the orange juice and sugar in a small saucepan and gently heat, stirring, until the sugar has dissolved. Turn off the heat and wait until the pan has cooled, then mix in the orange flower water.

Test whether or not the cake is ready by piercing with a fine skewer; if it comes out clean, the cake is cooked, if not, bake it for a few minutes longer.

Remove the cake from the oven and place it on a rimmed baking sheet. While warm, pierce the top of the cake all over with a skewer. Pour over the orange syrup, then cover the cake and set it aside to cool and soak up the syrup, a few hours or overnight.

Serve in slices with crème fraîche on the side.

# SALTED BUTTER CHEESECAKE COOKIES

These are really delicious, they're like a mini cheesecake but in cookie form.
(See photographs on pages 142 and 143.)

**SALTED BUTTER CHEESECAKE
FILLING**
25 g/1¾ tablespoons unsalted
butter
25 g/2 tablespoons dark brown
soft sugar
75 ml/⅓ cup double/heavy cream
¼ teaspoon sea salt flakes
100 g/½ cup minus 1 tablespoon
cream cheese (see page 16),
or use storebought

**SHORTBREAD COOKIES**
130 g/9 tablespoons salted butter,
softened
50 g/heaping ⅓ cup icing/
confectioner's sugar
½ teaspoon ground cinnamon
160 g/1½ cups plain/all-purpose
flour

MAKES 12

Make the salted butter sauce first as it needs time to cool. Add the butter, sugar, cream and salt to a saucepan set over a low-medium heat and whisk continuously for about 3 minutes as the ingredients gently melt and meld into one another. Once all the sugar has dissolved and the ingredients have combined, bring the mixture up to the boil and let bubble very vigorously for 2 minutes. Remove from the heat and let the bubbles subside. Set aside and let the cool.

To make the shortbread cookies, add the butter, sugar and cinnamon to a large mixing bowl, then briefly combine using an electric, hand-held whisk until well combined. Then add the flour until just combined and looking like chunky, fudgy crumbs.

Tip the mix onto a clean work surface and bring together with your hands into a log about 6 cm/2½ inches in diameter. You can handle it a little, but don't 'knead'; the butter will help bring everything together easily and if you handle the dough too much, you'll end up with tough shortbread. Transfer the log onto a large piece of parchment paper (or clingfilm/plastic wrap) and roll into a tight log, tying up both ends to seal. Transfer the log to the freezer for 20 minutes to firm up.

Preheat the oven to 180°C fan/200°C/400°F/gas 6.

Line your largest baking sheet with parchment paper, then take the cookie dough from the freezer. Unwrap the log, and slice it into discs 5 mm/¼ inch thick – you should get about 24. Lay them out on the baking sheet, transfer straight to the top shelf of the preheated oven and bake for 12–15 minutes, until sandy and slightly coloured at the edges. Place the baking sheet on a cooling rack and leave to cool.

Once the salted butter sauce has come down to room temperature, place the cream cheese in a mixing bowl and add 90 g/3 oz. sauce, mixing well to combine. Spread the filling onto the base of half the cookies, then top them with another cookie to create a filled sandwich cookie. Enjoy!

# DRINKS

# REFRESHING LEMON & MINT SODA

This fizzy lemonade made from fermented water kefir (see page 23) will forever change the way you think about soda! It's a hundred times tastier than all the commercial sodas out there and much better for you. Start this recipe 2 days before you want to enjoy it.

**4 tablespoons Water Kefir**
   **(see page 23)**
**100 g/½ cup raw cane sugar**
   **or other sweetener**
**1 litre/4 cups water, preferably**
   **non-chlorinated**
**1–2 organic lemons, peeled**
**a handful of fresh mint leaves**
**lemon slices and herb sprigs,**
   **to serve**
*1.5-litre/quart preserving jar*
   *with tight-fitting lid*
*plastic strainer*
*wooden or plastic spoon*
*1.5-litre/quart glass bottle*
   *or another 1.5-litre/quart*
   *preserving jar*

MAKES 1.5 LITRES/6 CUPS

Put the water kefir grains in the jar, add the sweetener and water and stir well. Cut each lemon into 8 slices and add to the jar together with the mint leaves. Seal with the jar lid. Keep the jar away from direct sunlight and leave to ferment for 2 days, stirring a couple of times in those 48 hours. Be careful when opening the jar because a considerable amount of carbon dioxide is produced by the fermentation.

Strain the liquid into a clean bottle or jar, squeeze out all the juice from lemon slices and add it, then discard the used lemon and mint leaves. Rinse the kefir grains and re-use. If you're not going to drink this soda right away, refrigerate and make sure it is well sealed to keep it fizzy. Serve with fresh lemon slices and garnish with a sprig of any herb you have to hand.

# VERY PINK YOGURT SMOOTHIE

This is a super-simple smoothie recipe made with only three basic ingredients. You can always make it a bit more filling if you like, by adding 1 tablespoon of either chia seeds, almond butter or nuts. It is light, refreshing, a little more on the sour side. Add more dates if you like it sweeter.

480 ml/2 cups yogurt (see page 13), or use storebought
130 g/1 cup raspberries or stoned/pitted sour cherries
60 g/2 oz. (approximately 6) Medjool dates, stoned/pitted

SERVES 2

In a high-speed blender, blend all ingredients until silky smooth. If you're using frozen fruit, thaw in advance. In summer, for a cool and refreshing smoothie, frozen fruits can be blended in directly.

A purple smoothie can be made by substituting raspberries or sour cherries with blueberries or blackberries; while a green version can be made adding one apple and 120 ml/½ cup green juice (made out of kale, chard, spinach, etc.). If you'd like a taste of the tropics, blend in mango, pineapple or papaya.

# COCONUT KEFIR SMOOTHIE

Fermented coconut water can be enjoyed by itself, but made into a delicious smoothie like this one, it's even tastier. Add coconut milk for a kick of coconut flavour, and while mango pairs wonderfully both in terms of taste and colour, other ripe and sweet fruits can be used too.

2 tablespoons water kefir (see page 23)
480 ml/2 cups coconut water
240 ml/1 cup full-fat coconut milk
1 fully ripe mango (approximately 340 g/12 oz.) or other ripe and sweet fruit
maple, rice or agave syrup, to taste (optional)
*1-litre/1-quart preserving jar with tight-fitting lid*

SERVES 2

Put the water kefir grains in the jar, add the coconut water and stir well. Cover it loosely or seal with the jar lid (sealing the jar will create more fizziness). Keep the jar away from direct sunlight and leave to ferment for 2 days, stirring a couple of times in those 48 hours. Taste the liquid – it should taste more sour than sweet. Strain the liquid into a blender jar, add the coconut milk and the mango flesh and blend until completely smooth. Taste and add a little maple, rice or agave syrup as necessary.

This probiotic smoothie can also be made with pineapple, strawberries or peaches. In hot weather, add some ice chips before blending.

# SPRING ONION & MISO TEA

As soon as you notice the first symptoms of a cold, make yourself a cup of this hot and salty tea. Miso will nourish you and alkalize your blood, and spring onion/scallion will boost circulation. Adding a little ginger juice just before drinking makes this tea even more powerful.

**1 teaspoon hatcho miso (see Tip)**
**240 ml/1 cup just-boiled water**
**2 spring onions/scallions,**
   **finely chopped**
**a small piece of fresh ginger**
   **(optional)**

SERVES 1

Dilute the miso in 2 tablespoons of just-boiled water. Add the spring onions/scallions and the remaining hot water. Grate the ginger, if using, and squeeze a few drops of juice in the tea. Stir and drink hot in small sips. If you don't have spring onions/scallions, use onion or leek.

**TIP** Hatcho miso made out of soybeans/soy beans, salt and koji starter, but other darker types, like miso pastes with added barley or rice can be used instead if you have no soy miso at hand.

# UME-SHO-KUZU DRINK

This healing drink is one of the most well-known Japanese-style remedies, and it is made using umeboshi plum, shoyu (Japanese natural soy sauce) and kuzu thickener (starch from a wild mountain root vegetable). It's magic in a cup, directly from nature!

**1/2 umeboshi plum, stoned/pitted**
**240 ml/1 cup water**
**1 teaspoon kuzu or arrowroot**
**a few drops of shoyu**
**a few drops of freshly squeezed**
   **ginger juice (optional)**

SERVES 1

Finely chop the umeboshi plum, place in a small saucepan and cover with the water. Bring to a slow boil and simmer for around 4 minutes. Dilute the kuzu or arrowroot in 2–3 teaspoons of cold water, add it to the saucepan, whisking constantly to avoid clumping, and simmer briefly until the liquid becomes translucent. Add the shoyu, let simmer for another 30 seconds and remove from the heat. Squeeze in a few drops of freshly squeezed ginger juice (if using), especially if you are trying to fight nausea or a stuffy nose.

Sip while hot and make a fresh portion each time. Drink 2–3 times per day for a couple of days. However, even 1 cup can make a big difference! Remember that all ingredients (except fresh ginger) have an almost indefinite shelf life so make sure you visit your local health-food store and buy the ingredients to have them at hand whenever needed!

# GINGER & LEMON KOMBUCHA

This brew is a healthy take on the classic ginger beer. It gets fizzy quickly which is infinitely satisfying and produces a kombucha brew with a complex flavour profile.

**1 tablespoon freshly juiced ginger or 1 tablespoon grated fresh ginger**
**freshly squeezed juice of ½ lemon**
**about 500 ml/2 cups unflavoured kombucha (see page 27)**
*a cold-press juicer (optional)*
*500-ml/2-cup capacity glass bottle with airtight lid*

SERVES 2–4

Simply add the ginger juice or grated ginger and lemon juice to the bottle, top up with unflavoured kombucha leaving a 1-cm/³⁄₈-inch air space at the top, then seal tightly.

Leave the sealed bottle at room temperature, out of direct sunlight, for 2–3 days. Refrigerate when the taste and fizz are to your liking. Strain if desired and serve cold.

# KOMBUCHA VIRGIN MARY

The vinegary tones enhance the tomato juice and spices no end. This makes a great alternative to alcohol as a Sunday morning pick-me-up. (See photograph on page 145.)

**100 ml/⅓ cup good-quality tomato juice**
**½–1 teaspoon Worcestershire sauce**
**5–10 drops of Tabasco, or other hot sauce**
**½ teaspoon horseradish sauce**
**a pinch of salt**
**2 grinds of black pepper, plus extra to serve**
**100 ml/⅓ cup basic kombucha (see page 27)**
**ice cubes, 1 celery stick/rib, a wedge of lime, to serve**

SERVES 1

Mix the tomato juice, Worcestershire sauce, Tabasco, horseradish, salt and pepper together in a jug/pitcher (or glass jar with a lid, given a good shake) before adding the kombucha.

Stir again before pouring over ice with an additional grind of pepper, a celery stick/rib and a wedge of lime. Serve immediately.

# BLUEBERRY LEMONADE

Here is a deliciously fruity drink made with a fermented kombucha tea base. The flavour combination of lemon and blueberry is a classic one, and makes for a refreshing and health-enhancing alternative to commercially made canned sodas.

**20 fresh or frozen blueberries**
**zest and freshly squeezed juice**
**   of ¼ lemon**
**about 500 ml/2 cups basic kombucha**
**   (see page 27)**
*1 x 500-ml/17-oz. capacity glass*
*   bottle with airtight lid*

SERVES 2–4

Add the lemon zest and juice and the blueberries to the bottle. If using fresh blueberries, squash them gently before adding to the bottle so the lovely blue colour is released into the kombucha.

Top up with the kombucha leaving a 1-cm/³⁄₈-inch air space at the top, then seal tightly.

Leave the sealed bottle at room temperature, out of direct sunlight, for 2–3 days, then refrigerate. Serve cold.

# CRANBERRY CLEANSE

If you are accustomed to ordering cranberry juice and lime when you are out at a bar with friends, you will be excited by this recipe, which is an enhanced version with additional health benefits to boot.

**200 ml/³⁄₄ cup cranberry juice**
**freshly squeezed juice of**
   **¹⁄₂ lime**
**2 litres/2 quarts basic kombucha**
   **(see page 27)**
**ice cubes, to serve**
*4 x 500-ml/17-oz. capacity glass*
   *bottles with airtight lids*

SERVES 8–16

Mix the cranberry juice with the lime juice and divide between the bottles. Top up with the kombucha leaving a 1-cm/³⁄₈-inch air space at the top, then seal tightly.

Leave the sealed bottles at room temperature, out of direct sunlight, for 2 days and refrigerate when the taste and fizz are to your liking. Serve cold over ice.

# APPLE & MINT COOLER

The combination of green apple and mint in this fermented kombucha tea tastes clean, clear and refreshing. Use a sour, crisp apple in the autumn/fall, such as Braeburn or Cox's for the best result.

**1 large apple or 150 ml/ ²/₃ cup**
   **fresh apple juice**
**4 large or 5 small fresh mint leaves**
**about 500 ml/2 cups basic kombucha**
   **(see page 27)**
*a cold-press juicer (optional)*
*1 x 500-ml/17-oz. capacity glass*
   *bottle with airtight lid*

SERVES 2–4

If using a large fresh apple, juice it in the cold-press juicer. It should yield around 150 ml/²/₃ cup of juice. If this is not possible, there are now a wonderful range of cloudy farm-apple juices available on the market distinguished by variety. Some are mixed with ginger, which will also be a tasty addition to your brew.

   Pour the apple juice into the bottle, add the mint leaves, top up with unflavoured kombucha leaving a 1-cm/³/₈-inch air space at the top, then seal tightly.

   Leave the sealed bottle at room temperature, out of direct sunlight for 2 days. Strain away the mint leaves if desired and refrigerate when the taste and fizz are to your liking.

   When ready to serve, pour into a jug/pitcher filled with ice. Add fizzy water to turn it into a refreshing spritz and enjoy.

# INDEX

## A

apples: apple & mint cooler 157
  wheatberry, apple & pecan salad 72
asparagus, pea & labneh salad 68
aubergines (eggplants): honey, miso & soy aubergine 118

## B

bagels, maple-sesame bacon & cream cheese 49
balsamic dressing 76
banana & blueberry kefir muffins 59
beef: reubens with beef, sauerkraut & Emmenthal 96
beetroot: beetroot, fig & grain salad 77
  beetroot latkes 46
black pepper ricotta sourdough toasts 55
blueberries: banana & blueberry kefir muffins 59
  blueberry lemonade 154
bread: croutons 67
  dukkah flatbreads 88
  eggy bread 53
  sourdough bread 31
  sourdough starter 28
  see also sandwiches; toast
brining vegetables 32
  broad bean, feta & dill salad 71
butter, caramelized 63
buttermilk 10
  buttermilk panna cotta 129
  crème fraîche 12
  feta-style cheese 20–1
  sour cream 11
butternut squash & chicory pasta bake 116

## C

cabbage: purple sauerkraut 38
  turmeric & chilli kimchi 37
cakes: carrot cake 138
  orange syrup semolina cake 140
capers, eggy bread with 53
caramelized butter 63
carrots: carrot cake 138
  carrot, coriander & caraway soup 67
  shredded carrot & courgette salad 80
  turmeric & chilli kimchi 37
chard: goat's cheese & chard tart 91
cheese: blue cheese dressing 119
  goat's cheese & chard tart 91
  loaded potato skins 84
  Parmesan crisps 64
  reubens with beef, sauerkraut & Emmenthal 96
  see also cottage cheese; cream cheese; feta; labneh; mascarpone; ricotta
chickpeas: roasted onion, tomato & chickpea curry 107
chicory: butternut squash & chicory pasta bake 116
chillies: pickled Scotch Bonnets 35
  turmeric & chilli kimchi 37
cloudberry coulis 129
coconut kefir smoothie 148
cod fillets, miso-marinated 111
coeur à la crème 133
cookies, salted butter cheesecake 141
cottage cheese 18
  spinach & cheese phyllo pie 104
courgettes (zucchini): orzo & roast courgette 115
  shredded carrot & courgette salad 80
crabcakes, kimchi 95
cranberry cleanse 155
cream: buttermilk panna cotta 129
  coeur à la crème 133
  cream cheese 16–17
  crème fraîche 12
  mascarpone 19
  sour cream 11
cream cheese 16–17
  coeur à la crème 133
  loaded potato skins 84
  maple-sesame bacon & cream cheese bagels 49
  salted butter cheesecake cookies 141
crème fraîche 12
  black garlic crème fraîche 87
croutons, sourdough 67
cucumber: chilled cucumber & mint soup 64
  cucumber pickles 35
  cucumber raita 107
curry: roasted onion, tomato & chickpea 107

## D

dressings: balsamic 76
  blue cheese 119
  hazelnut 77
  rich miso-tofu 41
  sesame miso 80
  vinaigrette 75
  yogurt 72
drinks: apple & mint cooler 157
  blueberry lemonade 154
  coconut kefir smoothie 148
  cranberry cleanse 155
  ginger & lemon kombucha 152
  kombucha 27
  kombucha Virgin Mary 152
  refreshing lemon & mint soda 147
  rejuvelac 26
  spring onion & miso tea 151
  ume-sho-kuzu drink 151
  very pink yogurt smoothie 148
dry-salting vegetables 32
dukkah flatbreads 88
dumplings, ricotta & spinach 108

## E F

eggplants see aubergines
eggs: eggy bread 53
  potato, pea, spring onion & feta frittata 92
  spicy kimchi hash browns 51
feta-style cheese 20–1
  broad bean, feta & dill salad 71
  potato, pea, spring onion & feta frittata 92
figs: beetroot, fig & grain salad 77
flatbreads, dukkah 88
frittata: potato, pea, spring onion & feta 92
frosting, mascarpone & lemon 138

## G

garlic: black garlic crème fraîche 87
  spicy leek & miso condiment 41
ginger: ginger & lemon kombucha 152
  pickled ginger 35

goat's cheese & chard tart 91
grapes: black pepper ricotta sourdough toasts 55

## H K

hash browns, spicy kimchi 51
hazelnuts: dukkah 88
  hazelnut dressing 77
honey, miso & soy aubergine 118
kefir: banana & blueberry kefir muffins 59
  coconut kefir smoothie 148
  milk kefir 24
  refreshing lemon & mint soda 147
  water kefir 23
kimchi: kimchi crabcakes 95
  kimchi pancake 87
  spicy kimchi hash browns 51
  turmeric & chilli kimchi 37
kombucha 27
  apple & mint cooler 157
  blueberry lemonade 154
  cranberry cleanse 155
  ginger & lemon kombucha 152
  kombucha Virgin Mary 152

## L

labneh 14
  asparagus, pea & labneh salad 68
  herbed labneh 88
  saffron & cardamom labneh 130
  za'atar labneh 103
lamb skewers 103
latkes, beetroot 46
leek & miso condiment 41
lemon: blueberry lemonade 154
  ginger & lemon kombucha 152
  refreshing lemon & mint soda 147

## M

mangoes: coconut kefir smoothie 148
  saffron & cardamom labneh 130
maple-sesame bacon & cream cheese bagels 49
mascarpone 19
  mascarpone & lemon frosting 138
  rhubarb & mascarpone tart 134
  spaghetti with gorgonzola, pecan & mascarpone

sauce 112
mayonnaise: sriracha mayo
95
yogurt dressing 72
milk: buttermilk 10
cottage cheese 18
cream cheese 16–17
milk kefir 24
ricotta 15
yogurt 13
millet: fermented millet
porridge 45
miso: fermenting vegetables
32
honey, miso & soy
aubergine 118
miso-marinated cod fillets
111
miso mushrooms on toast
54
rich miso-tofu dressing 41
sesame miso dressing 80
spicy leek & miso
condiment 41
spring onion & miso tea
151
muffins, banana & blueberry
kefir 59
mushrooms: fermented
pearl barley, mushroom &
walnut salad 75
miso mushrooms on toast
54
tofu noodles 123

N O
noodles, tofu 123
onion, tomato & chickpea
curry 107
orange syrup semolina cake
140
orzo & roast courgette 115

P
pancake, kimchi 87
panna cotta, buttermilk 129
Parmesan crisps 64
passion fruit: coeur à la
crème 133
pasta: butternut squash &
chicory pasta bake 116
orzo & roast courgette 115
spaghetti with gorgonzola,
pecan & mascarpone
sauce 112
pearl barley: fermented pearl
barley, mushroom & walnut
salad 75
saffron shrimp with
fermented pearl barley
pilaf 124
pears: spelt, pear &
prosciutto salad 76

peas: asparagus, pea &
labneh salad 68
eggy bread with 53
potato, pea, spring onion &
feta frittata 92
pecan nuts: spaghetti with
gorgonzola, pecan &
mascarpone sauce 112
wheatberry, apple & pecan
salad 72
peppers (bell): lamb skewers
103
roasted red pepper,
pomegranate & sumac
raita 83
pickles 34–5
cucumber pickles 35
pickled ginger 35
pickled Scotch Bonnets 35
pies: sour cream raisin pie
137
spinach & cheese phyllo pie
104
pilaf, fermented pearl barley
124
pomegranate: roasted red
pepper, pomegranate &
sumac raita 83
porridge, fermented millet
45
potatoes: beetroot latkes 46
loaded potato skins 84
potato, pea, spring onion &
feta frittata 92
spicy kimchi hash browns
51
prawns (shrimp): saffron
shrimp 124
prosciutto: spelt, pear &
prosciutto salad 76
purple sauerkraut 38

Q R
quinoa: beetroot, fig & grain
salad 77
radicchio, roasted 119
raisins: sour cream raisin pie
137
raita: cucumber raita 107
roasted red pepper,
pomegranate & sumac
raita 83
raspberries: very pink yogurt
smoothie 148
rejuvelac 26
reubens with beef,
sauerkraut & Emmenthal 96
rhubarb & mascarpone tart
134
ricotta 15
black pepper ricotta
sourdough toasts 55
ricotta & spinach

dumplings 108
rye flour: sourdough starter
28

S
saffron & cardamom labneh
130
saffron shrimp 124
salads: asparagus, pea &
labneh 68
beetroot, fig & grain 77
broad bean, feta & dill 71
fermented pearl barley,
mushroom & walnut 75
shredded carrot &
courgette 80
spelt, pear & prosciutto 76
wheatberry, apple & pecan
72
salt: brining vegetables 32
dry-salting vegetables 32
salted butter cheesecake
cookies 141
sandwiches: fried tofu
sandwiches 96
reubens with beef,
sauerkraut & Emmenthal 96
sauerkraut: purple
sauerkraut 38
reubens with beef,
sauerkraut & Emmenthal
96
scallions see spring onions
Scotch Bonnets, pickled 35
semolina cake, orange syrup
140
sesame miso dressing 80
sesame seeds: dukkah 88
shortbread: rhubarb &
mascarpone tart 134
salted butter cheesecake
cookies 141
shoyu, fermenting
vegetables 32
smoked salmon, beetroot
latkes with 46
smoothies: coconut kefir
smoothie 148
very pink yogurt smoothie
148
soups: carrot, coriander &
caraway 67
chilled cucumber & mint 64
spinach yogurt 63
sour cream 11
chilled cucumber & mint
soup 64
sour cream raisin pie 137
sourdough bread 31
sourdough starter 28
spaghetti with gorgonzola,
pecan & mascarpone sauce
112

spelt berries: rejuvelac 26
spelt, pear & prosciutto
salad 76
spinach: ricotta & spinach
dumplings 108
spelt, pear & prosciutto
salad 76
spinach & cheese phyllo pie
104
spinach yogurt soup 63
spring onions (scallions):
loaded potato skins 84
potato, pea, spring onion &
feta frittata 92
spring onion & miso tea 151
sriracha mayo 95
strawberries: coeur à la
crème 133

T
tarts: goat's cheese & chard
tart 91
rhubarb & mascarpone tart
134
tea: kombucha 27
toast: black pepper ricotta
sourdough toasts 55
miso mushrooms on toast
54
tofu: fried tofu sandwiches 96
rich miso-tofu dressing 41
tofu noodles 123
tomatoes: cherry tomato
sauce 108
kombucha Virgin Mary 152
lamb skewers 103
roasted onion, tomato &
chickpea curry 107
turmeric & chilli kimchi 37

U V W
ume-sho-kuzu drink 151
vegetables, fermenting 32
vinaigrette dressing 75
water kefir 23
wheat berries: beetroot, fig
& grain salad 77
wheatberry, apple & pecan
salad 72

Y Z
yogurt 13
cucumber raita 107
labneh 14
roasted red pepper,
pomegranate & sumac raita
83
spinach yogurt soup 63
very pink yogurt smoothie
148
yogurt dressing 72
za'atar labneh 103
zucchini see courgettes

# RECIPE CREDITS

**VAL AIKMAN-SMITH**
Spicy kimchi hash browns

**LOUISE AVERY**
Apple & mint cooler
Blueberry lemonade
Cranberry cleanse
Ginger & lemon kombucha
Kombucha virgin Mary

**CHLOE COKER & JANE MONTGOMERY**
Fermented barley, mushroom & walnut salad

**MEGAN DAVIES**
Black pepper ricotta & bay-roasted grape sourdough toasts
Butternut squash & chicory pasta bake
Carrot, coriander & caraway soup with sourdough croûtons
Eggy bread with capers & petit pois
Goat's cheese & chard tart
Honey, miso & soy aubergine with yogurt & coriander
Loaded potato skins
Maple-sesame bacon & cream cheese bagels
Miso mushrooms on toast
Potato, pea, spring onion & feta frittata
Roasted onion, tomato & chickpea curry with cucumber raita
Salted butter cheesecake cookies
Tofu noodles with mushrooms & marmite

**AMY RUTH FINEGOLD**
Saffron shrimp with fermented barley pilaf
Shredded carrot & courgette salad with sesame miso dressing
Spelt, pear & prosciutto salad
Wheatberry, apple & pecan salad

**TONIA GEORGE**
Reubens with beef, sauerkraut & Emmenthal

**DUNJA GULIN**
Banana & blueberry kefir muffins
Coconut kefir smoothie
Fermented millet porridge
Fermented vegetables
Fried tofu sandwiches with pickles
Kombucha
Milk kefir
Purple sauerkraut
Refreshing lemon & mint soda
Rejuvelac
Rich miso-tofu dressing
Sourdough bread
Sourdough starter
Spicy leek & miso condiment
Spring onion & miso tea
Turmeric & chilli kimchi
Ume-sho-kuzu drink
Very pink yogurt smoothie
Water kefir

**JENNY LINFORD**
Asparagus, pea & labneh salad
Beetroot latkes with smoked salmon & crème fraiche
Broad bean, feta & dill salad
Buttermilk
Buttermilk panna cotta with cloudberry coulis
Carrot cake with mascarpone & lemon frosting
Chilled cucumber & mint soup with Parmesan crisps
Coeur a la crème with strawberries & passion fruit
Cottage cheese
Cream cheese
Crème fraiche
Dukkah flatbreads with herbed labneh
Feta-style cheese
Kimchi pancake with black garlic crème fraiche
Labneh
Lamb skewers with za'atar labneh
Mascarpone
Orange syrup semolina cake with crème fraiche
Rhubarb & mascarpone tart
Ricotta
Ricotta & spinach dumplings with cherry tomato sauce
Roasted red pepper, pomegranate & sumac raita
Saffron & cardamom labneh with mango
Sour cream
Sour cream raisin pie
Spaghetti with gorgonzola, pecan & mascarpone sauce
Spinach & cheese phyllo pie
Spinach yogurt soup with caramelized butter
Yogurt

**THEO A. MICHAELS**
Beetroot, fig & grain salad with feta & hazelnut dressing
Roasted radicchio with blue cheese dressing

**JAMES PORTER**
Cucumber pickles
Kimchi crab cakes with sriracha mayo
Miso-marinated cod fillets
Pickled ginger
Pickled Scotch bonnets

**SHELAGH RYAN**
Orzo & roast courgette with semi-dried tomato dressing

# PHOTOGRAPHY CREDITS

**PETER CASSIDY**
Page 83.

**JONATHAN GREGSON**
Page 98.

**MOWIE KAY**
Pages 34, 76, 78, 79, 88, 101, 110, 120 & 121.

**ERIN KUNKEL**
Pages 51 & 146.

**DAVID MUNNS**
Page 71.

**STEVE PAINTER**
Pages 50, 79 & 104.

**RITA PLATTS**
Pages 2, 4, 5, 52, 85, 117, 122, 142 & 143.

**WILLIAM REAVELL**
Pages 74 & 97.

**NASSIMA ROTHACKER**
Page 53.

**CHRISTOPHER SCHOLEY**
Pages 37 & 68.

**TOBY SCOTT**
Pages 9, 22, 23, 24, 25, 26, 27, 29, 30, 33, 36, 39, 40, 44, 58, 99, 149 & 150.

**IAN WALLACE**
Pages 72, 84, 112, 118, 119, 124 & 147.

**KATE WHITAKER**
Pages 55, 59, 103, 114 & 140.

**CLARE WINFIELD**
Pages 1, 3, 6, 7, 8, 10, 11, 12, 13, 14, 15, 16, 17, 18, 19, 20, 21, 27, 28, 32, 42, 43, 47, 48, 49, 54, 56, 57, 60, 61, 62, 63, 64, 65, 66, 69, 70, 73, 81, 82, 86, 87, 89, 90, 93, 95, 100, 102, 105, 106, 109, 113, 125, 126, 127, 128, 129, 130, 131, 132, 133, 135, 136, 139, 144, 145, 152, 153, 154, 155, 156 & 157.